GR

Michael Swan
David Baker

GRAMMAR SCAN

Diagnostic tests for
Practical English Usage
Third Edition

OXFORD
UNIVERSITY PRESS

OXFORD
UNIVERSITY PRESS

Great Clarendon Street, Oxford OX2 6DP

Oxford University Press is a department of the University of Oxford. It furthers the University's objective of excellence in research, scholarship, and education by publishing worldwide in

Oxford New York

Auckland Cape Town Dar es Salaam Hong Kong Karachi Kuala Lumpur Madrid Melbourne Mexico City Nairobi New Delhi Shanghai Taipei Toronto

With offices in

Argentina Austria Brazil Chile Czech Republic France Greece Guatemala Hungary Italy Japan Poland Portugal Singapore South Korea Switzerland Thailand Turkey Ukraine Vietnam

OXFORD and OXFORD ENGLISH are registered trade marks of Oxford University Press in the UK and in certain other countries

First published 2008

2012 2011 2010 2009 2008
10 9 8 7 6 5 4 3 2 1

ISBN: 978 0 19 442272 7 TESTS BOOK
ISBN: 978 0 19 442274 1 TESTS PACK

Printed in China

Contents Summary

Introduction

What are these tests?

They are **diagnostic tests**, designed to be used with ***Practical English Usage* (Third Edition).**

They will help you to check what you know, and what you don't know, about English grammar and usage. By using these tests you can discover what you need to learn, and where to find the necessary explanations.

The tests are at three levels:
- **Upper Intermediate** (29 tests)
- **Advanced** (29 tests)
- **Expert** (30 tests)

Each test has questions on one general area of grammar or usage (for example 'past and perfect tenses', 'adjectives', 'articles', 'confusable words').

Using the tests

You can use these tests to check your knowledge of a particular area of grammar or usage. For instance, to find out how much you know about the use of **passives**:
- Choose the level (for example **Upper Intermediate**) that you think is right for you.
- Go to the test on **passives** at that level (Test 9).
- Answer the questions.
- Check your answers in the key at the back of the book.
- If you get some answers wrong, the answer key will show you where in ***Practical English Usage*** **(Third Edition)** you can find the explanations you need for each point.
- Go to ***Practical English Usage*** **(Third Edition)** and read the explanations.
- Try the test again, preferably a few days later, and see if you can now get more or less everything right.

Levels

You don't need to choose the same level for all the tests. You may, for example, know enough about present tenses to do the Advanced test, but find that the Upper Intermediate test is better suited to your knowledge of prepositions.

If you find a test too easy or difficult, try a higher or lower level for that language point. If most of the Upper Intermediate tests are too hard for you, it may be best to wait until later before using the book. If you can do all the Expert-level tests without difficulty, congratulations: you have a remarkable knowledge of English, and don't need the book!

Correctness: not too little, not too much

Not everybody needs the same level of correctness in a foreign language.

- Some people just need a practical working knowledge of English in order to be able to communicate reasonably successfully. However, if they make too many mistakes with the most common structures, they can be difficult to understand. The **Upper Intermediate tests** will help with problems at that level.
- Other language learners and users need quite a high level of correctness for their studies or work, especially if they need to write English. They will find the **Advanced tests** useful.
- Absolute correctness in a foreign language is generally unnecessary, and out of reach of most adult learners. But some very advanced students may want their English to be as free from error as possible. The **Expert-level tests** are designed for such learners. These tests will also be useful for non-native-speaking teachers of English.

Remember: grammar is not the only part of a language that has to be learnt and practised; it is not even the most important part. Don't get obsessed with correctness; otherwise you will end up just learning grammar instead of learning English. Use this book sensibly, in moderation, to help you meet your own personal needs.

Two important notes for teachers

1. These are **diagnostic** tests, not grading tests or attainment tests. Their function is **not** to assign students to levels, to enable you to give students marks for their work, or to draw an imaginary line between 'success' and 'failure'. They are not appropriate tools for such purposes, and we should be sorry if our book was used in these ways. The tests are best used for syllabus planning: to check learners' strengths and weaknesses in particular linguistic areas, so as to show what still needs to be taught. They will help you to answer questions like 'What problems do my students still have with basic tense use?', 'Are they having trouble with relative clauses?' or 'Do they know enough about spoken grammar?'
2. Testing can be an easy option for teachers; and because of this, teachers can be tempted to spend too much time on tests. Bear in mind that teaching time is limited, and testing is not teaching. Asking people what they know doesn't teach them anything very much; it simply tells you what they may need to learn.

Upper Int

LEVEL 1

Upper Intermediate

LEVEL 1 Upper Intermediate

1 verb forms and their names

1 What is another name for *progressive*?

A. conditional ☐
B. perfect ☐
C. continuous ☒
D. infinitive ☐

2 Which of these are NOT the names of English verb forms?

A. simple past ☐
B. present progressive ☐
C. future perfect ☐
D. perfect present ☒
E. simple progressive ☒
F. past perfect ☐
G. future past ☒

3 Choose the correct name from the box for each verb form. (You won't need to use all of them.)

> (simple) future   future progressive   future perfect
> future perfect progressive   present perfect   present progressive
> simple present

A. is singing ...present progressive...
B. will have explained ...future perfect...
C. will arrive ...simple future...
D. works ...-//- present...
E. will be playing ...future progressive...
F. will have been studying ...future perfect progressive...

4 Choose the correct name from the box for each verb form. (You won't need to use all of them.)

> past perfect   past perfect progressive   past progressive
> present perfect   present perfect progressive   simple past
> simple present

A. was talking ...past progressive...
B. had telephoned ...past perfect...
C. stopped ...simple past...
D. has seen ...present perfect...
E. had been waiting ...past perfect progressive...
F. has been waiting ...present -//-...

▶

5 Are these verb forms active A, passive P or wrong W?

A. was invited P
B. was starting A
C. were sent P
D. were been talking W
E. has given P
F. is being written P
G. has been working A
H. will been studying W
I. had writing W
J. will be asked P
K. will be working A

6 Choose the correct name from the box for each passive verb form. (You won't need to use all of them.)

future progressive   infinitive   past perfect   past progressive
present perfect   present perfect progressive   present progressive
simple past   simple progressive

A. had been expected past perfect
B. to be heard infinitive
C. was being cleaned past progressive
D. is being watched simple progressive
E. has been told present perfect
F. was sold simple past

7 Are these forms normal N, unusual U or wrong W?

A. How long **has** this work **been being done**? U
B. She **will be being interviewed** tomorrow morning. [illegible]

8 In the text, find one modal verb, one infinitive, one passive verb and one third-person singular form.

I can't see my brother as often as I want. His wife hates me for some reason, so I am only invited to their house once a year at Christmas.

A. modal verb can
B. infinitive see
C. passive verb invited
D. third-person singular form hates

9 In the text, find two auxiliary verbs, one past participle and one prepositional verb.

What have you done with that book that I was looking at when you arrived?

A. auxiliary verbs have, was
B. past participle done
C. prepositional verb looking at

2 present and future verbs

1 Write the third person singular forms of these verbs, e.g.
work → *works* .

A. stay *stays*
B. reply *replies*
C. push *pushes*
D. complete *completes*
E. hurry *hurries*

F. pull *pulls*
G. catch *catches*
H. enjoy *enjoys*
I. examine *examines*

2 Are these spellings right R or wrong W? Correct the ones that are wrong.

A. I'm **siting** at the back of the train. — *W* *sitting*
B. He's **travelling** this week. — *R*
C. Is this train **stoping** in Birmingham? — *W* *stopping*
D. She's **showing** the new design to her manager. — *R*
E. I'm **hopping** she'll arrive on time. — *W* *hoping*
F. My sister is always **beatting** me at tennis. — *W* *beating*
G. It's **beginning** to rain. — *R*
H. We're **developping** a new product. — *W* *developing*

3 Say the words aloud. One word in each list has a different vowel sound. Which word?

A. stays, pays, says, rains — /seɪz/
B. does, goes, knows, throws

4 Which of these present tense forms is/are correctly used?

A. What **are** frogs usually **eating**? ☒
B. The kettle **boils**. ~ Please take it off the stove. ☒
C. Water **boils** at 100° Celsius. ☑
D. I'**m playing** tennis every Wednesday. ☒ *play*
E. Alice **works** for an insurance company. ☑
F. Look – it **snows**! ☒ *is snowing*

5 Which of these sentences is/are possible?

A. Fred **works** as a waiter. ☑
B. Fred **is working** as a waiter. ☑

6 Choose the best reply: A or B.
Why do you work so hard?

A. ~ Because I'm only happy when I'm busy. ☑
B. ~ Because I have to finish my report by the end of this week. ☐ ▶

7 Which of these sentences is/are possible?

A. My dishwasher doesn't work. ☑
B. My dishwasher isn't working. ☑
C. My dishwasher won't start. ☑

8 Right or wrong?

A. **I'm liking** this wine very much.
B. Of course **I'm believing** you!
C. **I'm knowing** her very well.

9 Which of these answers is/are possible: A, B or both?

Excuse me. How do I get to the station?

A. ~ **You go** straight on to the traffic lights, then **you turn** left. ☑
B. ~ **You're going** straight on to the traffic lights, then
 you're turning left.

10 A TV chef is describing a recipe as she's cooking it. Which sentence(s) is/are possible: A, B or both?

A. First **I take** a bowl and **break** two eggs into it. ☑
B. First **I'm taking** a bowl and **am breaking** two eggs into it. ☒

11 Is this exchange right or wrong? If it's wrong, correct it.

How long do you know her? ~ I know her since 1980.

How long have you know him?

12 Which is the correct reply: A, B or C?

Remember to phone me when you arrive.

A. ~ Yes, I do. ☒
B. ~ Yes, I'm going to. ☒
C. ~ Yes, I will. ☑

13 Which is the best reply: A or B?

Do you see those clouds?

A. ~ Yes. It'll rain. ☑
B. ~ Yes. It's going to rain. ☑

14 Which of these sentences is/are right?

A. His train **will arrive** at 11.30. ☐
B. His train **arrives** at 11.30. ☑
C. The summer term **starts** on April 10th. ☐
D. The summer term **will start** on April 10th. ☐

15 Which is the correct continuation: A or B?

The roads are icy.

A. Be careful while **you're** driving home tomorrow. ☑
B. Be careful while **you'll be** driving home tomorrow. ☐

3 past and perfect verbs

1 Write the past tenses of these verbs, e.g.
ask → asked .

A. start started
B. stop stopped
C. plan planned
D. develop developed
E. care cared
F. hurry hurried
G. offer offered
H. stun stunned
I. panic panicked
J. regret regretted

2 Are these verb forms right R or wrong W? If any are wrong, correct them.

A. I **payed** him in cash. W paied
B. I'm afraid I've **hit** your car. R
C. She **learnt** it. R
D. The hot water pipes **burst** last night. R
E. I've never **rode** a horse before. W ridden
F. She's never **flown** in a helicopter before. R
G. The film **begun** ten minutes ago. W began
H. Wait! I've **forgot** my keys. W forgotten
I. She realised she had **went** the wrong way. W gone
J. The horse has **fell** at the first fence. W fallen
K. They **flew** to Argentina on Sunday. R
L. He **lied** in his bed all morning. W lay

3 Are the spellings of these *-ing* forms right or wrong? If any are wrong, correct them.

A. He was **hopeing** to leave school next year. W hoping
B. They've been sailing and **canoeing**.
C. She's been **lying**.
D. I think he's been **dying** his hair.
E. He was **offerring** to help with the gardening.
F. The police were **preventing** people from entering the building.
G. The horse was **gallopping** away from the field.

4 The past ending *-ed* is pronounced in the same way in each word in the list except one. Find the odd one out.

A. lived, tried, passed, failed, lied.
B. hoped, missed, laughed, cried, worked.
C. started, finished, ended, heated, landed.

▶

5 Which of these questions is/are correct?

A. Who did you phone? ☐
B. Who phoned you? ☐
C. Who phoned? ☐
D. Who did phone? ☐

6 Right or wrong?

A. **I've decided** to go to the party. ___
B. **John's decided** to go to the party. ___
C. **John and I have** decided to go to the party. ___
D. **John and I've** decided to go to the party. ___

7 Which sentence ending(s) is/are right?
When I got up this morning ...

A. ... the birds **were singing**. ☐
B. ... the birds **sang**. ☐
C. ... I **was having** breakfast. ☐
D. ... I **had** breakfast. ☐

8 Right or wrong?

A. I **rang** the bell six times. ___
B. I **rung** the bell six times. ___
C. I **was ringing** the bell six times. ___

9 Right or wrong?

A. She realised I was joking. ___
B. She said she realised I was joking. ___
C. She said she was realising I was joking. ___

10 Is the reply right or wrong? If it's wrong, correct it.

Do you know Africa well? ~ Yes, I've travelled there a lot. ___

....

11 Which continuation(s) is/are possible: A, B or both?
Andy has won a big prize!

A. **He's won** €50,000 in the Euro Lottery. ☐
B. **He won** €50,000 in the Euro Lottery. ☐

12 Which of these is/are right: A, B or both?

A. My friends **helped** me a lot since I lost my job. ☐
B. My friends **have helped** me a lot since I lost my job. ☐

13 If the answer is ~ *since March*, which of these questions is/are right?

A. How long **are** you here for? ☐
B. How long **were** you here for? ☐
C. How long **have you been** here for? ☐

▶

14 Which sentence ending(s) is/are possible?
She's been working there ...

A. ... **for** a long time. ☐
B. ... **since** a long time. ☐
C. ... **until** a long time. ☐

15 Right or wrong?

A. I asked Anne to call me at 10.30. Did she phone today? ___
B. I haven't heard from Bill since yesterday. Has he phoned today? ___

16 Which of these questions is/are right?

A. Why **have not you** booked your holiday yet? ☐
B. Why **haven't you** booked your holiday yet? ☐
C. Why **have you not** booked your holiday yet? ☐

17 Right or wrong?

A. I've been playing a lot of tennis recently. ___
B. I've played tennis three times this week. ___

18 Which of these questions is/are possible?

A. How long **did you know** her? ☐
B. How long **have you known** her? ☐
C. How long **have you been knowing** her? ☐

19 Is this opening sentence of a children's story right or wrong? If it's wrong, correct it.

Once upon a time, a beautiful young girl has lived in a forest with her grandmother. ___

....

4 auxiliary verbs

1 Right R or wrong W?

A. I **have to** go now. ___
B. **I've got to** go now. ___
C. I **must** go now. ___

2 Which of these auxiliary verbs is/are used correctly?

A. You **must** do your homework before you watch TV. ☐
B. You **are to** do your homework before you watch TV. ☐
C. You **must** have tea with us before you go home. ☐
D. You **are to** have tea with us before you go home. ☐

▶

3 Is this sentence right or wrong? If it's wrong, correct it.

I did never believe you were lying. ____

....

4 Add one word to this sentence to make it sound more natural.

She thinks I don't love her, but I love her.

....

5 Which of these expressions can end the sentence correctly?

My wife loves dancing ...

A. ... and I. ☐
B. ... and so do I. ☐
C. ... and so do I love dancing. ☐
D. ... and I do too. ☐

6 Right or wrong?

Are you having ...

A. ... a bad day? ____
B. ... a headache? ____
C. ... any brothers or sisters? ____

7 Which of these replies is/are possible?

Has your sister got a car?

A. ~ No, she doesn't have got. ☐
B. ~ No, she hasn't got. ☐
C. ~ No, she hasn't got one. ☐
D. ~ No, she hasn't one. ☐

8 Right or wrong?

Have you got a credit card? It's important .... one if you're travelling abroad.

A. to have ____
B. to have got ____

9 Right or wrong?

I'm going to .... my hair cut this afternoon.

A. get ____
B. have ____
C. make ____

5 modal verbs (1): *can, could, may, might*

1 What is the difference between these two requests?

A. **Can** I have some more tea, please?
B. **Could** I have some more tea, please?

....

2 *Can, could* or both?

A. STATION PORTER: .... I help you?
B. PASSENGER: Yes. .... you tell me where Platform 14 is, please?

3 *Can, could* or both?

What shall we do tomorrow? ~ Well, we .... go fishing.

4 Which verb form(s) can complete the sentence correctly?
She .... be at home. I'll phone home and find out.

A. can't ☐
B. may not ☐
C. might not ☐

5 Is this sentence right R or wrong W? If it's wrong, correct it.

He **could borrow** my car if he'd asked. ⌴

....

6 Which replies can be used?
Has anyone seen Susan?

A. ~ Yes, **I see** her coming now. ☐
B. ~ Yes, **I'm seeing** her coming now. ☐
C. ~ Yes, **I can see** her coming now. ☐

7 Who is more likely to be going to London tomorrow?
JOE: I **may** be going to London tomorrow.
MARY: I **might** be going to London tomorrow.

A. Joe. ☐
B. Mary. ☐
C. We don't know. ☐

8 Which expression(s) can end the sentence?
She lives in France; that's why...

A. ... she **can** speak French. ☐
B. ... she **may** speak French. ☐

9 *Could, might* or both?

When I was young, people .... smoke in the office.

6 modal verbs (2): *will, would, used to, must, should, ought*

1 Are these company notices right R or wrong W?

A. *ALL EMPLOYEES **WILL** COMPLETE WEEKLY TIMESHEETS.* ___

B. *ALL EMPLOYEES **MUST** COMPLETE WEEKLY TIMESHEETS.* ___

2 A host is greeting his guests. Which is the best way to complete the sentence?

Thanks for coming, Mary. And you .... Mary's husband. I've heard a lot about you.

A. are ☐

B. should be ☐

C. must be ☐

3 What does this sentence mean?

Liverpool **should** win the cup this year.

A. I think Liverpool will definitely win. ☐

B. I think Liverpool will very probably win. ☐

4 Which verb means the same as *don't have to* here?

You **don't have to** work tomorrow if you don't want to.

A. mustn't ☐

B. needn't ☐

C. shouldn't ☐

5 Right or wrong?

A. Fred, you **should** go home now: it has started to snow. ___

B. Fred **should** be home soon; he left the office at six. ___

6 Right or wrong? If wrong, write the correct form.

A. He oughts to understand. ___

....

B. Do we ought to go now? ___

....

C. She ought see a dentist. ___

....

7 Right or wrong?

I **ought to** call you yesterday, but I'm afraid I forgot. ___ ▶

8 Which expression(s) can end the sentence correctly?
There isn't much time; ...

A. ... you **have better listen** to me. ☐
B. ... you **had better listen** to me. ☐
C. ... you **had better listening** to me. ☐
D. ... you **had better to listen** to me. ☐

9 Which is more usual: A or B?

A. You **hadn't better** get home late from the party tonight. ☐
B. You**'d better not** get home late from the party tonight. ☐

10 Right or wrong?

A. I **use to** smoke 20 cigarettes a day but I really want to give up soon. ____
B. I **used to** smoke 20 cigarettes a day but I gave up three years ago. ____

7 structures with infinitives

1 Choose the right verb form(s) to complete the sentences correctly.

A. You seem .... (*to work, working, to be working*) harder than usual this month.
B. Why's she so late? She can't still .... (*work, to work, be working, to be working*).

2 Choose the right verb form(s) to complete the sentences correctly.

A. I'm sorry not .... (*to come, have come, to have come*) on Thursday.
B. You should .... (*told, have told, to have told*) me you were coming today.

3 Which sentence is normal N, which is unusual U and which is wrong W?

A. Try **to not** be late. ____
B. Try **not to** be late. ____
C. Try **to don't be** late. ____

4 *Carry, to carry* or both?

A. I watched her .... her bags from the baggage hall.
B. 'Could you help me .... my bags to the taxi rank?' she asked.
C. In the end, she let me .... all three of her bags. ▶

5 Which verb form(s) can complete the question correctly?
You look tired. Why not ______ a holiday?

A. take ☐
B. to take ☐
C. taking ☐

6 Which of these verbs can be followed by an infinitive?

A. agree ☐
B. expect ☐
C. enjoy ☐
D. like ☐
E. start ☐
F. finish ☐
G. think ☐
H. suggest ☐
I. manage ☐
J. regret ☐
K. give up ☐
L. remember ☐

7 Right R or wrong W?

A. She wanted **that I write** to her. ___
B. She wanted **I write** to her. ___
C. She wanted **me to write** to her. ___

8 Right or wrong?

A. He's the oldest athlete **who has ever won** an Olympic gold medal. ___
B. He's the oldest athlete **ever to win** an Olympic gold medal. ___

9 Right or wrong?

A. I'd like something **that will stop** my toothache. ___
B. I'd like something **to stop** my toothache. ___
C. Did you tell her which pills **she should take**? ___
D. Did you tell her which pills **to take**? ___

10 Right or wrong?

A. I don't know **what to say**. ___
B. I wonder **who to ask**. ___
C. I can't decide **whether to reply**. ___

11 Which of these is/are possible?

A. **What should we do** if there's a fire? ☐
B. **What to do** if there's a fire? ☐
C. [*COMPANY NOTICE*]: ***WHAT TO DO*** *IF FIRE BREAKS OUT* ☐

12 Which verb phrase(s) can finish the sentence correctly?
When it was my turn, I stood up ______
(*to speak, for to speak, for speaking*). ▶

13 Which of these sounds more natural?

A. To read documents carefully before signing them is very important. ☐
B. It is very important to read documents carefully before signing them. ☐

14 Which expression(s) can end the sentence correctly?
I'm very happy ...

A. ... **to** help you. ☐
B. ... **for the company to** help you. ☐
C. ... **for they to** help you. ☐
D. ... **that they can** help you. ☐

15 Is this sentence right or wrong? If it's wrong, correct it.

Is there anybody for Louise to play with in the village? ___

....

8 *-ing* forms and past participles

1 Right R or wrong W?

Knowing not what to do, I went home. ___

2 Right or wrong?

A. 'Does **my smoking** annoy you?' asked Fred. ___
B. **Fred's smoking** really annoyed her. ___
C. **He smoking** really annoyed her. ___
D. **His smoking** really annoyed her. ___

3 Which word(s) can complete the question correctly?

Do you mind .... (*them, their, they*) smoking?

4 *Meeting, to meet* or both?

It was so nice .... you.

5 Which of these verbs can be followed by an *-ing* form?

A. avoid ☐
B. hope ☐
C. suggest ☐
D. give up ☐
E. want ☐
F. decide ☐
G. expect ☐
H. delay ☐
I. put off ☐
J. agree ☐

6 *To smoke, smoking* or both?

At last I've managed to stop ....

▶

7 Choose the right verb form(s) to complete the sentences: *-ing* form, infinitive or both. (Both options may be possible.)

A. I**'ve finished** .... (*reading, to read*) the book you recommended.
B. I**'ve given up** .... (*smoking, to smoke*).
C. I **enjoy** .... (*learning, to learn*) foreign languages.
D. I **like** .... (*speaking, to speak*) foreign languages.
E. I **hope** .... (*seeing, to see*) you again soon.

8 Which verb form(s) can complete the sentence correctly?
I like the idea .... to the seaside.

A. moving ☐
B. of moving ☐
C. to move ☐

9 Choose the right verb form(s) to complete the sentences: *-ing* form, infinitive or both.

A. Before .... (*starting, to start*) your car, always check the mirrors.
B. He's talking about .... (*finding, to find*) another job.
C. You mustn't drive your car without .... (*insuring, to insure*) it first.

10 Choose the right verb form(s) to end the replies: *-ing* form, infinitive or both.

A. Can I give you a lift? ~ No, **I'd prefer** .... (*walking, to walk*).
B. Did you drive to work? ~ No, **I prefer** .... (*walking, to walk*).

11 Right or wrong?

A. As she walked out, she was smiling. ☐
B. She walked out smiling. ☐

12 Which is the right word for each gap?

I was really .... (*interesting, interested*) in the film I saw yesterday, but the complicated plot made me .... (*confusing, confused*).

9 passives

1 Which two replies sound most natural?

Are the windows still dirty?

A. ~ No, I've cleaned them. ☐
B. ~ No, they've been cleaned. ☐
C. ~ No, they've been cleaned by me. ☐

2 Which of these sentences would work better in an academic article?

A. **People have written** too many books about the Second World War. ☐
B. Too many books **have been written** about the Second World War. ☐
C. **I have not yet analysed** the results of the experiment. ☐
D. The results of the experiment **have not yet been analysed**. ☐

3 Which of these verb forms can be used in English?

A. to have been invited ☐
B. being watched ☐
C. having been told ☐
D. having be spoken to ☐
E. being looked at ☐

4 Are the passive forms right R or wrong W?

My husband is preparing lunch now.

A. Lunch **is prepared** now. ___
B. Lunch **is being prepared** now. ___
C. Lunch **is preparing** now. ___

5 Are the passive forms right or wrong?

The company has promoted Bill.

A. Bill **is promoted** by the company. ___
B. Bill **has promoted** by the company. ___
C. Bill **has been promoted** by the company. ___

6 Right or wrong?

A. **We were questioning** by the police for several hours. ___
B. **We were put** in the police cells overnight. ___
C. In the morning, **we have released**. ___

7 Change the sentences into passive sentences with the same meaning, e.g.

She gave her sister the car. → Her sister was given the car.

A. The bank sent me a new chequebook.

....

B. We pay them a lot of money for doing very little.

....

C. They will never tell us the real truth.

....

▶

8 Right or wrong?

A. I was told **to wait** outside the station at six o'clock. ☐
B. I was told **to be waiting** outside the station at six o'clock. ☐
C. She is expected **to be released** today. ☐
D. He is thought **to have escaped** last night. ☐

9 Somebody has paid for your meal in a restaurant. Which passive sentence is right: A, B or C?

A. Has been paid for your meal. ☐
B. Your meal has been paid. ☐
C. Your meal has been paid for. ☐

10 verbs: some special structures

1 Adjectives or adverbs? Choose the right word to complete these sentences.

A. This cheese tastes .... (*good, well*)
B. This cheese goes .... (*good, well*) with wine.
C. Bungee jumping looks .... (*dangerous, dangerously*) to me.
D. She always looks .... (*careful, carefully*) at fruit before she buys it.

2 Which word(s) can complete the sentence correctly?

The forecast says it will .... colder tomorrow.

A. become ☐
B. get ☐
C. change ☐
D. grow ☐
E. turn ☐

3 Which of these questions is/are possible?

A. Who was it **sent**? ☐
B. Who was it **sent to**? ☐
C. Who did you **give it**? ☐
D. Who did you **give it to**? ☐

4 Right R or wrong W?

A. I **gave John** the keys. ☐
B. I **explained Laura** the problem. ☐
C. **Make me** a cup of coffee, please. ☐
D. Can you **teach me** the guitar next year? ☐
E. Can you **describe me** the man who attacked you? ☐

▶

5 Right or wrong?

A. She switched **off the light**. ⌴
B. She switched **the light off**. ⌴
C. She switched **it off**. ⌴
D. She switched **off it**. ⌴

6 Which of these is more common?

A. Can you lend your bike to my brother? ☐
B. Can you lend my brother your bike? ☐

7 Right or wrong?

A. She sent some flowers to the nurse. ⌴
B. She sent to the nurse some flowers. ⌴
C. She sent the nurse some flowers. ⌴

8 Which sounds more natural?

A. What are you thinking about? ☐
B. About what are you thinking? ☐

9 Right or wrong?

A. Listen! ⌴
B. Listen to! ⌴
C. Listen me! ⌴
D. Listen to me! ⌴
E. You never listen me. ⌴
F. You never listen to me. ⌴

11 nouns

1 Are the plural forms right R or wrong W? (If they're wrong, correct them.)

A. The children rode **donkeys** on the beach. ⌴ ....
B. I love going to **parties** and hate staying at home. ⌴ ....
C. A cat is said to have nine **lifes**. ⌴ ....
D. Are we having **sandwichs** for lunch? ⌴ ....
E. The **rooves** of the buildings were covered in snow. ⌴ ....
F. They all wore football **scarfs** with their team colours. ⌴ ....

2 Do these words have one 1 or two 2 syllables?

A. clothes ⌴
B. crashes ⌴
C. knives ⌴
D. houses ⌴

▶

3 How is the plural ending pronounced: -s (as in *say*), -z (as in *zoo*) or -ɪz (as in *quiz*)?

A. plate**s** ___
B. knive**s** ___
C. garage**s** ___
D. house**s** ___
E. dream**s** ___
F. cloth**s** ___
G. cloth**es** ___
H. bridge**s** ___

4 Complete the table.

Male	Female
A. host	....
B. bridegroom	....
C. waiter	....
D. policeman	....
E.	heroine
F.	nun
G.	widow

5 Right or wrong?

A. A lot of social problems **is** caused by unemployment. ___
B. Half of his students **don't** understand a word he says. ___
C. Some of these people are members of the club and the rest **are** guests. ___

6 Choose which word(s) can complete the sentences: the first option, the second option or both.

A. I have some important .... (*information, informations*) for you.
B. They are buying .... (*furniture, furnitures*) for their new flat.
C. 'Buck' is .... (*a slang, slang*) for 'dollar'.
D. Did you bring all your gardening .... (*tool, tools*) with you?
E. We've made some important .... (*progress, progresses*) with the building work.
F. You need breathing .... (*equipment, equipments*) if you're going diving.
G. John, who is the police's main suspect, has black .... (*hair, hairs*)
H. If you're going to the shops, please buy some .... (*spaghetti, spaghettis*). ▶

7 Which option(s) can complete the sentence correctly?
My .... been lost.

A. baggage has ☐
B. baggages have ☐
C. suitcase has ☐
D. suitcases have ☐

8 Which of these is/are possible?
A pair of ...

A. ... shoes ☐
B. ... trousers ☐
C. ... earrings ☐
D. ... glasses ☐
E. ... scissors ☐

9 Which sentence is more formal: A or B?

A. Let's **talk** about your plans. ☐
B. Let's **have a talk** about your plans. ☐

10 Is the use of apostrophes (') right R or wrong W?

A. my parents' house ___
B. mens' clothes ___
C. the children's room ___
D. Mr Harris's car ___
E. the people next doors' dog ___
F. the Smiths' new house. ___

11 Which of these sentences is/are right?

A. She's a cousin of John's. ☐
B. She's a John's cousin. ☐
C. She's one of John's cousins. ☐
D. Is this the boss's car? ☐
E. Is this the John's car? ☐

12 What is *milk chocolate*?

A. A kind of milk. ☐
B. A kind of chocolate. ☐

▶

13 Which of these questions is/are possible?

A. Is there **a shoes shop** near here? ☐
B. Are there any **shoe shops** near here? ☐
C. Are there any **shoes shops** near here? ☐
D. Is there **a ticket office** near here? ☐
E. Is there **a tickets office** near here? ☐
F. Are there any **tickets offices** near here? ☐
G. The town holds a **horses race** every month. ☐
H. The town holds **horse races** every month. ☐
I. The town holds **horses races** every month. ☐

14 Do *a coffee cup* and *a cup of coffee* sometimes mean the same?

....

15 Which of these is/are possible?

A. a flower bunch ☐
B. a paper piece ☐
C. a wine glass ☐
D. a cards pack ☐
E. a steak knife ☐
F. a butter dish ☐
G. a paint tin ☐

12 pronouns

1 Are the replies right R or wrong W?
Who said that?

A. ~ It was her. ___
B. ~ Her. ___
C. ~ She did. ___
D. ~ She. ___

2 Are these sentences right or wrong? (If they're wrong, correct them.)

A. He hated ties because reminded him of his school uniform. ___

....

B. I picked up the coins and put in my pocket. ___

....

C. Have some olives. ~ No, thanks. I don't like. ___

....

▶

3 Which of these replies is/are possible?
Who's that over there?

A. ~ **It's** John Cook. ☐
B. ~ **He's** John Cook. ☐
C. ~ **It's** my mother. ☐
D. ~ **She's** my mother. ☐

4 Which of these sentences is/are right?

A. My sister's nearly as tall as **me**. ☐
B. My sister's nearly as tall as **I am**. ☐
C. My brother can run faster than **me**. ☐
D. My brother can run faster than **I can**. ☐

5 Which is the more polite option in each case?

A. *[at home]*
CHILD: .... (*Dad, He*) said I could go out.
DAD: No, I didn't!

B. *[at the scene of an accident]*
MAN: .... (*This lady, She*) needs an ambulance.
WOMAN: No, really. I'm all right.

C. *[in a shop]*
SHOPKEEPER: Would .... (*you, she*) like anything else?
CUSTOMER: No, that's all, thank you.

6 Which of these pronouns are used correctly?

A. I burnt **me** on the hot pan. ☐
B. I burnt **myself** on the hot pan. ☐
C. Here's ten dollars. Get **you** something to eat. ☐
D. Here's ten dollars. Get **yourself** something to eat. ☐
E. He gave **me** money for lunch. ☐
F. He gave **myself** money for lunch. ☐

7 When Mary sent a letter of complaint to the company, the company president wrote to her herself.
Are these statements true T, false F or we don't know ??

A. The company president is a woman. ___
B. The company president didn't ask somebody else to write the letter. ___
C. The sentence could also be written:
... the company president herself wrote to her. ___

8 *Myself, by myself* or both?

A. I like to spend time ....
B. I can do it .... ; I don't need any help.

▶

9 Is this sentence right or wrong? If it's wrong, correct it.

My mother and her sister are very close: they talk **to themselves** almost every day. ____

....

10 Which option(s) can complete the sentence correctly?

Peter has a room and Julia has a room. The children both have .... rooms.

A. their own ☐
B. themself's ☐
C. themselves' ☐

11 Are these sentences right or wrong? If they're wrong, correct them.

A. There's **somebody** outside who wants to speak to you. ____

....

B. There are **somebody** outside who want to speak to you. ____

....

12 Choose the right option(s) for each sentence.

A. I hope my new boss is .... (*a nice somebody, somebody nice*).
B. Would you like .... (*else, something else*) to eat?
C. ~ Yes, I fancy .... (*a sweet something, something sweet*).

13 Which is the best reply: A, B or C?

Which of these are your suitcases?

A. ~ They're **the blue suitcases** with the red straps. ☐
B. ~ They're **the blue ones** with the red straps. ☐
C. ~ They're **the blue** with the red straps. ☐

14 Right or wrong?

A. If you haven't got **a fresh chicken**, I'll take **a frozen**. ____
B. If you haven't got **a fresh chicken**, I'll take **a frozen one**. ____
C. If you haven't got **fresh cream**, I'll take **tinned**. ____
D. If you haven't got **fresh cream**, I'll take **tinned one**. ____

15 Right or wrong?

A. **Which** would you like? ____
B. **Which one** would you like? ____
C. **Which ones** would you like? ____
D. **This** looks the best. ____
E. **This one** looks the best. ____
F. **Either one** will suit me. ____
G. **This small** looks the nicest. ____
H. **This small one** looks the nicest. ____

▶

16 **They** say the police arrested my friends.
Who are 'They'?

A. the police ☐
B. the speaker's friends ☐
C. other people ☐

13 determiners (1): articles, possessives and demonstratives

1 I hope your children aren't scared of my dogs.
Can this sentence mean the same: yes Y or no N?

I hope your children aren't scared of **the dogs**. ___

2 Right R or wrong W?

A. **A doctor** must like people. ___
B. **Doctor** must like people. ___
C. **Doctors** must like people. ___
D. **The doctors** must like people. ___

3 If necessary, take out *a/an* from these sentences. (They may not all need to be changed.)

A. It's **a** very hot day today.
B. It's **a** very hot today.
C. I'm so happy to have you as **a** friend.
D. I'm so happy to have you as **a** my friend.
E. I haven't got **a** money for the taxi. Can you lend me some?
F. Have we got **a** plan to deal with this situation?

4 If necessary, add *a/an* to these sentences. (They may not all need to be changed.)

A. She's engineer working in the oil industry.

....

B. Don't go out in the sun without hat.

....

C. The factory uses energy supplied from solar power.

....

D. Don't use your plate as ashtray.

....

5 *Students, some students* or both?

A. Our next-door neighbours are ....
B. I was talking to .... at the party. ▶

6 If necessary, take out *the* from these sentences. (They may not all need to be changed.)

A. **The** life has been hard for him since he came to this country.
B. I'm writing a book on **the** life of Mozart.
C. I didn't understand **the** nature of **the** problem.
D. I love **the** nature, so I really don't like living in **the** city.

7 Which sentence ending(s) are possible?
Life would be much quieter without ...

A. ... mobile phone. ☐
B. ... mobile phones. ☐
C. ... the mobile phone. ☐

8 Choose the right options in each sentence.

A. He goes .... (*to school, to the school*) every day .... (*by bus, by the bus*).
B. I walk .... (*by school, by the school*) every day on my way .... (*to work, to the work*).
C. They sent her .... (*to prison, to the prison*) for six months.
D. Her parents visited her .... (*at prison, at the prison*) every week.
E. I work in a shop .... (*by day, by the day*) and study .... (*at night, at the night*).

9 Which of these sentences is/are right?

A. **Europe's economic problems** are serious. ☐
B. **The Europe's economic problems** are serious. ☐
C. **The economic problems of Europe** are serious. ☐
D. I met **boss's wife** yesterday. ☐
E. I met **the boss's wife** yesterday. ☐

10 Right or wrong?

A. I want to learn how to play **the guitar**. ____
B. I want **the guitar** lessons. ____

11 Which of these sentences is/are right?

A. **Both children** are good at maths. ☐
B. **Both the children** are good at maths. ☐
C. I haven't seen her **all week**. ☐
D. I haven't seen her **all the week**. ☐
E. **All three brothers** were arrested. ☐
F. **All the three brothers** were arrested. ☐

▶

12 Right or wrong?

A. I'll see you **on Thursday**. ____
B. I'll see you **next Thursday**. ____
C. I'll see you **on the next Thursday**. ____
D. I'll see you **on the Thursday before New Year's Day**. ____

13 Right or wrong?

A. **The** Queen welcomed **the** President. ____
B. **The** Queen Elizabeth welcomed **the** President Kennedy. ____

14 Can these exclamations begin with *What ...*, *What a ...* or both?

A. .... lovely dress you're wearing today!
B. .... lovely weather we've been having recently!
C. .... rubbish you're talking, Martin!

15 Which of these should begin with the definite article? Write in *The* if necessary.

A. .... Philippines
B. .... California
C. .... Thames
D. .... Oxford Street
E. .... Oxford University
F. .... British Museum

16 Which is better: *her* or *the*?

A. The ball hit her on .... head.
B. Katy broke .... arm mountain climbing.
C. She stood there, ... hands in .... pockets.

17 *Its, it's, whose* or *who's*?

A. .... baby is that? ~ Do you mean the one .... crying?
B. What's the dog doing? ~ .... playing with .... bone.

18 Right or wrong?

A. Put **those old newspapers** down – they're dirty. ____
B. Put **those** down – they're dirty. ____
C. Tell **those people** to go away. ____
D. Tell **those** to go away. ____

▶

19 Right or wrong?

A. Can I get you anything else? ~ No, **this** is all, thank you. ⌴
B. OK, **that's** it! I'm leaving. It was nice knowing you. ⌴

20 *This* or *that* (in a British English telephone call)?

A. Hello. .... is Elizabeth. Is .... Ruth?
B. ~ Yes, ... is Ruth speaking.

14 determiners (2): other determiners

1 Which of these sentences is/are possible?

A. I'll take **all two** shirts, please. ⌴
B. I'll take **all three** shirts, please. ⌴
C. I'll take **all the three** shirts, please. ⌴

2 Choose the right option(s). (More than one may be possible for each sentence.)

A. .... (*All, All of*) my friends like riding.
B. .... (*All, All of*) children can be difficult.
C. All .... (*we, us, of us*) can come tomorrow.
D. Mary sent her love to .... (*all them, all of them, them all*).

3 Right R or wrong W?

A. Are you going to stay here **all the night**? ⌴
B. Are you going to stay here **all the time**? ⌴

4 Which of these expressions is/are used correctly?

A. **Everybody** stood up. ☐
B. **Everyone** stood up. ☐
C. **All** stood up. ☐
D. **All people** stood up. ☐
E. **All the people** stood up. ☐

5 Right or wrong?

A. I like **all** music. ⌴
B. I like **every** music. ⌴
C. I like **all kinds of** music. ⌴
D. I like **every kind of** music. ⌴

▶

6 Which expression(s) can complete the sentence correctly?
She works here .... except Sundays.

A. all day ☐
B. all the days ☐
C. all days ☐
D. every day ☐

7 Right or wrong?

A. She's drunk **all the** orange juice. ___
B. She's drunk **the whole** orange juice. ___
C. She's eaten **all a** loaf of bread. ___
D. She's eaten **a whole** loaf of bread. ___

8 Which is the most natural continuation?
Eating too much sugar is bad for you.

A. Ask **all dentists.** ☐
B. Ask **any dentist.** ☐
C. Ask **every dentist.** ☐

9 Which replies are possible?
Did you get the oil?

A. ~ No, there **wasn't any** left. ☐
B. ~ No, there **wasn't some** left. ☐
C. ~ No, there **was none** left. ☐
D. ~ No, there **wasn't none** left. ☐

10 Which host sounds more polite: A or B?

A. Would you like **some** more meat? ☐
B. Would you like **any** more meat? ☐

11 Right or wrong?

A. She's eaten **both** chops. ___
B. She's eaten **the both** chops. ___
C. She's eaten **both the** chops. ___
D. She's eaten **both of** chops. ___
E. She's eaten **both of the** chops. ___

12 Right or wrong?

A. **Both** the children have gone to bed. ___
B. The children have **both** gone to bed. ___
C. The children have gone to bed **both**. ___

13 Which is more normal here: *has* or *have*?

Each of us .... a serious problem.

▶

14 Which option(s) can complete this sentence correctly?

There's a meeting .... six weeks.

A. all ☐
B. all the ☐
C. each ☐
D. every ☐

15 *Little, a little, few* or *a few*?

A. The average politician has .... real power.
B. .... people can speak a foreign language really fluently.
C. Would you like .... soup?
D. Only .... students in my class are studying two foreign languages.
E. '.................... knowledge is a dangerous thing.' [saying]

16 Who is most keen to move house and who is least keen?

A. 'I can think of **few** reasons to move house.' ☐
B. 'I can think of **a few** reasons to move house.' ☐
C. 'I can think of **quite a few** reasons to move house.' ☐

Most keen: .... **Least keen:** ....

17 Are these sentences right or wrong? If they are wrong, correct them.

A. Lots of patience **are needed** to learn to teach small children. ____

....

B. A lot of my friends **wants** to emigrate. ____

....

18 Right or wrong?

A. I need **more two** loaves of bread. ____
B. I need **two more** loaves of bread. ____
C. I need **another two** loaves of bread. ____

19 Are these uses of *most* right or wrong?

A. **Most** children like ice cream. ____
B. **The most** children like ice cream. ____
C. **Most of** children like ice cream. ____
D. The Romans conquered **most of** Europe. ____
E. The Romans conquered **the most of** Europe. ____

20 Which of these uses of *neither* is/are right?

A. **Neither brother** is married. ☐
B. **Neither of brothers** is married. ☐
C. **Neither of her brothers** is married. ☐

▶

21 Right or wrong?

A. You're **so beautiful.** ☐
B. You're **so much beautiful.** ☐
C. You're **so much more beautiful** than me. ☐

22 *Some* or *any*?

A. Could you please give me .... advice?
B. You never give me .... advice.
C. We got there without .... trouble.

23 Which word(s) can end this sentence correctly?
He's so selfish: he never thinks of ...

A. ... others. ☐
B. ... other people. ☐
C. ... others people. ☐
D. ... another. ☐
E. ... the other. ☐

15 adjectives and adverbs

1 Choose the right option to complete each sentence correctly.

A. My sister Jill is two years .... (*elder, older*) than me.
B. I think that fish you caught is still .... (*live, alive*).

2 The baby's asleep. *Right*
~~An asleep baby.~~ *Wrong*

Which of these adjectives follow the same pattern?

A. afraid ☐
B. alive ☐
C. alone ☐
D. angry ☐
E. awake ☐
F. awful ☐

3 Right R or wrong W?

A. The wall is **two metres high.** ☐
B. My brother is **ten years older** than me. ☐
C. Your house is **thousands of dollars worth** more than mine. ☐
D. The path is **two kilometres long.** ☐

4 Can you improve these sentences by taking out the highlighted words: yes Y or no N?

A. Let's go somewhere **that is** quiet. ☐
B. The most important **thing** is to be happy. ☐

▶

5 Which adjectives are in the right order?

A. a **green wine** bottle ☐
B. **dancing leather** shoes ☐
C. a **political old** idea ☐
D. the **latest educational** reform ☐
E. a **cool lovely** drink ☐
F. **green beautiful** mountains ☐
G. that **fat silly** cat ☐

6 Which is normal: A, B or C?

A. He was tall and dark and handsome. ☐
B. He was tall, dark and handsome. ☐
C. He was tall, dark, handsome. ☐

7 Right or wrong?

A. He's collecting money for **the blind**. ____
B. **The tired** went to bed and the rest of us sat up talking. ____
C. **The old** deserve to be looked after when they need help. ____

8 Which of these is/are right?

A. **The French** are usually very patriotic. ☐
B. **A French** is usually very patriotic. ☐
C. **A Frenchman** is usually very patriotic. ☐

9 Is the word *loaf* necessary in this sentence: yes or no?

I'd like two large loaves and one small **loaf**. ____

10 Which of these is/are possible?

A. **Stupidly**, I forgot my keys. ☐
B. I **stupidly** forgot my keys. ☐
C. I forgot my keys **stupidly**. ☐

11 Which of these sentences is/are right?

A. I **never** ask her about her marriage. ☐
B. **Never** I ask her about her marriage. ☐
C. **Never** ask her about her marriage. ☐

12 Right or wrong?

A. Here comes your bus. ____
B. Here your bus comes. ____
C. Here it comes. ____
D. Here comes it. ____

▶

13 Right or wrong?

A. **Every day** I have a shower. ⎵

B. **Daily** I have a shower. ⎵

14 Right or wrong?

A. Don't throw out of the window orange peel. ⎵

B. Don't throw orange peel out of the window. ⎵

15 Is this sentence right or wrong? If it's wrong, correct it.

Put the butter in the fridge at once. ⎵

....

16 Right or wrong?

A. **Usually** I take the train to work. ⎵

B. I **usually** take the train to work. ⎵

C. I take **usually** the train to work. ⎵

17 Which of these sentences is/are normal?

A. **Hardly** it matters. ☐

B. It **hardly** matters. ☐

C. It matters **hardly**. ☐

D. **Almost** it was dark. ☐

E. It was **almost** dark. ☐

F. It was dark **almost**. ☐

16 comparison

1 Write in the comparatives and superlatives of these adjectives.

	Adjective	Comparative	Superlative
A.	fat	....	....
B.	thin	....	....
C.	large	....	....
D.	small	....	....
E.	good	....	....
F.	bad	....	....
G.	happy	....	....
H.	simple	....	....
I.	quiet	....	....
J.	intelligent	....	....

2 Which word(s) can complete the sentence correctly?

Today's hotter .... yesterday.

A. as ☐

B. than ☐

C. that ☐

▶

3 Which word(s) can complete the sentence correctly?
Mary's .... of the three girls.

A. the taller ☐
B. the tallest ☐
C. tallest ☐

4 Right R or wrong W?

A. I'm getting **more and more fat.** ___
B. I'm getting **fatter and fatter.** ___
C. We're going **more and more slowly.** ___
D. We're going **more slowly and more slowly.** ___

5 Right or wrong?

A. Your room is **even untidier** than your brother's. ___
B. Your room is **even more untidy** than your brother's. ___

6 Which of these sentences is/are normally right?

A. He sings better than **she.** ☐
B. He sings better than **her.** ☐
C. He sings better than **she does.** ☐
D. She doesn't sing as well as **he.** ☐
E. She doesn't sing as well as **him.** ☐
F. She doesn't sing as well as **he does.** ☐

7 Which expression(s) can end the request correctly?
Could you all ...

A. ... be more quiet, please? ☐
B. ... be quieter, please? ☐
C. ... talk more quietly, please? ☐
D. ... talk quietlier, please? ☐

8 Which expression(s) can end the sentence correctly?
She's the fastest player ...

A. ... **in** the team. ☐
B. ... **of** the team. ☐
C. ... **in** them all. ☐
D. ... **of** them all. ☐

9 Which word(s) can complete the sentence?
Your new flat is .... nicer than mine.

A. much ☐
B. very ☐
C. very much ☐
D. far ☐
E. a lot ☐

17 prepositions

1 Put the words in the right order to make informal spoken questions.

A. looking at what you are

....?

B. general which on is flight the travelling

....?

C. films in kind interested what of you are

....?

2 Right R or wrong W?

A. She went home **without to say** goodbye. ☐
B. She went home **without saying** goodbye. ☐
C. He **asked for** a loan. ☐
D. He **asked to borrow** some money. ☐
E. He **asked for to borrow** some money. ☐

3 Choose the right preposition. (X = no preposition.)

A. Are you any good .... (*at, in, with*) tennis?
B. Congratulations .... (*at, for, on*) your new job!
C. Who's the woman dressed .... (*in, of, with*) green?
D. Excuse me, sir. You haven't paid .... (X, *for, of*) your drink.

4 *To, with* or both?

A. Be **polite** .... your parents.
B. Be **nice** .... your sister.
C. Be **kind** .... your children.

5 Right or wrong?

A. I got **into** the car. ☐
B. I got **onto** the bus. ☐
C. I got **off** the car. ☐
D. I got **off** the bus. ☐

6 Choose the right preposition for each sentence.

A. Brie is an example .... (*for, from, of*) a French soft cheese.
B. Brie is typical .... (*for, from, of*) French soft cheeses.

7 *To, with* or no preposition X ?

A. Her marriage .... Philip didn't last long.
B. How long have you been married .... him?
C. She married .... her first boyfriend.

▶

8 Choose the right preposition for each sentence.

A. Please fill in the form ………… (*by, in, with*) black or blue ink.
B. She looks much younger ………… (*from, in, on*) her wedding photos.
C. There's a mistake ………… (*at, in, on*) page 120.

9 Choose the right preposition for each gap in the sentence.
The meeting started at 2.00. Sally arrived at 1.50 and Jim arrived at exactly 2 o'clock.

Sally arrived ………… (*at, in, on*) time and Jim arrived ………… (*at, in, on*) time.

10 Which of these sentences is/are right (in informal English)?

A. See you next Monday. ☐
B. Come any day you like. ☐
C. The party lasted all night. ☐

11 Right or wrong?

A. Take these pills **three times a day**. ____
B. Take these pills **three times in a day**. ____

12 Which of these sentences is/are correct (in informal speech)?

A. What time does Granny's train arrive? ☐
B. What day is your hair appointment? ☐

13 *At, in* or *on*?

A. She works ………… a big insurance company.
B. I don't think he's ………… his office.
C. There's a big spider ………… the ceiling.
D. There's no room ………… the bus.
E. What time do we arrive ………… New York?

14 Add the correct time prepositions.

A. I'll meet you at the match ………… Saturday afternoon ………… 2.30.
B. I work best ………… the morning and I never work ………… night.
C. Come and see us ………… Christmas.
D. Come and see us ………… Christmas Day.

15 Choose the right options.

I killed the spider by ………… (*hit, hitting*) it ………… (*by, with*) a shoe. ▶

16 ***For, during* or both?**

A. My father was in hospital .... six weeks.
B. I used to visit him .... an hour or two .... the afternoon.

17 ***During, in* or both?**

A. We'll be on holiday .... August this year.
B. We'll be on holiday .... the whole of August this year.
C. I'll try to phone you .... the meeting.

18 **Right or wrong?**

A. I'll have tea **instead of** coffee, please. ☐
B. No, I won't have coffee; I'll have tea **instead of**. ☐

19 ***Like, as* or both?**

A. She's good at scientific subjects .... physics.
B. He's very .... his father.
C. He looks so handsome, ... his father.
D. He worked .... a waiter for two years.
E. Nobody knows her .... I do.

20 **Choose the right option for each sentence.**

A. There's a fire station .... (*in front of, opposite*) my house.
B. The woman .... (*in front of, facing*) me in the post office queue was taking a long time.
C. The bosses sat on one side of the table .... (*in front of, facing*) the union leaders on the other side.

18 questions, negatives and exclamations

1 **Right** R **or wrong** W**?**

A. When was your reservation made? ☐
B. Where are staying the President and his family? ☐

2 **Which of these are normal questions?**

A. Who did phone just now? ☐
B. What sort of music does make you happy? ☐
C. What sort of music does your mother like? ☐

▶

3 Which of these replies sound(s) rude?

When does the film start?

A. ~ How should I know? ☐
B. ~ How would I know? ☐
C. ~ How can I find out? ☐

4 Are these sentences right or wrong? If they're wrong, correct them.

A. It is important to don't worry. ___

....

B. The best thing about a holiday is to not work. ___

....

5 Right or wrong?

A. He does never work. ___
B. He hardly ever works. ___
C. He doesn't hardly ever work. ___

6 Which of these questions is/are correct?

A. **Why haven't they** replied to my emails yet? ☐
B. **Why they have not** replied to my emails yet? ☐
C. **Why have they not** replied to my emails yet? ☐
D. **Doesn't she have** any friends to help her? ☐
E. **Hasn't she** any friends to help her? ☐

7 SPEAKER 1: **Did** you go and see Helen yesterday?
SPEAKER 2: **Didn't** you go and see Helen yesterday?

Which statement is correct?

A. Speaker 1 expects the answer 'Yes.' ☐
B. Speaker 2 expects the answer 'Yes.' ☐
C. We don't know whether either speaker expects the answer 'Yes.' ☐

8 Which meaning of each reply is correct: A or B, C or D?

Haven't you written to Mary?

A. ~ Yes. (= I have written to her.) ☐
B. ~ Yes. (= I haven't written to her.) ☐

Didn't you go to work this morning?

C. ~ No. (= I went to work.) ☐
D. ~ No. (= I didn't go to work.) ☐

9 Right or wrong?

A. Be careful! ___
B. Do be careful! ___
C. Don't be silly! ___

▶

10 Which of these sentences is/are right?

A. **Always remember** what I told you. ☐
B. **Remember always** what I told you. ☐
C. **Never speak** to me like that again! ☐
D. **Speak never** to me like that again! ☐

11 Which of these exclamations is/are right?

A. How nice! ☐
B. How it is cold! ☐
C. How cold it is! ☐
D. How beautifully you sing! ☐
E. How you sing beautifully! ☐
F. How have you grown! ☐
G. How you've grown! ☐

12 Is this sentence right or wrong? If it's wrong, correct it.

What a beautiful smile has your sister! ___

....

13 Are these exclamations right or wrong? If they're wrong, correct them.

A. What rude man! ___ ....
B. What beautiful weather! ___ ....

19 conjunctions

1 Is the comma (,) in each sentence necessary N or unnecessary U?

A. If you are passing, come in and see us. ___
B. Come in and see us, if you are passing. ___

2 Right R or wrong W?

A. She was depressed, **because didn't know what to do.** ___
B. She was depressed, **and didn't know what to do.** ___
C. She was depressed, **because she didn't know what to do.** ___

3 Are the replies right or wrong?
I'm going out, Mum.

A. ~ You can go as soon as you've brushed your hair. ___
B. ~ As soon as you've brushed your hair. ___

4 Which of these sentences is/are right?

A. I liked him, **so** I tried to help him. ☐
B. **Because** I liked him, I tried to help him. ☐
C. **Because** I liked him, **so** I tried to help him. ☐

▶

5 Choose the right options. (More than one might be possible.)

A. That's the girl ______ (*that, who*) works with my sister.
B. August 31st is a national holiday ______ (*that, when*) everybody dances in the streets.
C. The house ______ (*that, where*) I live is very small.

6 Which of these fixed expressions is/are right?

A. If you're hungry, have some **bread and butter**. ☐
B. Do you want your tea in a mug or a **saucer and cup**? ☐
C. Can you use chopsticks, or would you prefer a **fork and knife**? ☐

7 Which option(s) can complete the sentence correctly?
It looks ______ it's going to rain.

A. if ☐
B. as if ☐
C. as though ☐
D. like ☐

8 *I* or *I'll*?

A. I'll remember that day **as long as** ______ live.
B. I'll telephone you **before** ______ arrive.

9 These meetings can last as long as four hours.
What does this sentence mean?

A. These meetings must not last longer than four hours. ☐
B. It's possible for these meetings to last four hours, which is a very long time. ☐

10 He's not only nice, but also clever.
He's clever as well as nice.

Do the two sentences mean the same: yes Y **or no** N**?** ___

11 *Because, because of* or both?

A. We were late ______ it rained.
B. We were late ______ the rain.
C. We were late ______ you.
D. We were late ______ I met you.

12 Do the pairs of sentences mean the same: yes or no?

A. I finished early **because** I worked fast.
Because I worked fast, I finished early. ___
B. He did military service **before** he went to university.
Before he did military service, he went to university. ___

▶

13 Right or wrong?

A. Don't forget to call your mother **before you leave** this afternoon. ☐
B. *PLEASE PUT OUT ALL LIGHTS* ***BEFORE LEAVING*** *THE OFFICE.* ☐

14 Right or wrong?

A. It doesn't matter whether we go by bus or train, it'll take at least six hours. ☐
B. Whether we go by bus or train, it'll take at least six hours. ☐

15 Which sounds better in these situations: *if* or *whether*?

A. *[in a shop]* I can't decide .... I prefer the blue dress or the red one. What do you think?
B. *[in a newspaper]* The Finance Minister has not yet decided .... she will recommend a tax cut or an increase in public spending.

20 *if*

1 Which of these sentences is/are right?

A. I'll meet you on the tennis court at 10.00 if it isn't raining. ☐
B. I'd be happier if I had more friends. ☐
C. It had been nice if she had said 'Thank you.' ☐
D. I visit my mother on Saturdays if I have time. ☐
E. If Mary didn't phone this morning, she's probably away. ☐

2 Which of these sentences is/are right?

A. If I see him, I'll tell him. ☐
B. If I'll see him, I'll tell him. ☐
C. I'll tell him when I see him. ☐
D. I'll tell him when I'll see him. ☐

3 Right R or wrong W?

A. If I **know** her name, I'd tell you. ☐
B. If I **knew** her name, I'd tell you. ☐
C. If I**'d know** her name, I'd tell you. ☐

4 Which of these sentences is/are right?

A. If you **asked** me, I would have told you. ☐
B. If you **had asked** me, I would have told you. ☐
C. If you **would have asked** me, I would have told you. ☐

5 Right or wrong?

A. I don't know if **I'm** ready in time. ☐
B. I don't know if **I'll be** ready in time. ☐

▶

6 Is this sentence right or wrong? If it's wrong, correct it.

If I **were** rich, I would take more holidays. ☐

7 Who is probably the faster runner: Speaker A or Speaker B?

A. 'If I **win** this race ...' ☐
B. 'If I **won** this race ...' ☐

8 Which three of these continuations sound most natural?

Are you free on Wednesday night? ...

A. ... **If you are free**, let's meet at 7. ☐
B. ... **If you are**, let's meet at 7. ☐
C. ... **If yes**, let's meet at 7. ☐
D. ... **If so**, let's meet at 7. ☐
E. ... **If you aren't free**, let's meet on Thursday. ☐
F. ... **If not**, let's meet on Thursday. ☐
G. ... **If no**, let's meet on Thursday. ☐

9 If she won't come to us, ... we'll have to go and see her.
Which word(s) can fill the gap correctly?

A. then ☐
B. therefore ☐
C. so ☐

21 indirect speech

1 Is the indirect speech right R or wrong W? If it's wrong, correct it.

DIRECT: 'Where is the money?'
INDIRECT: We asked where the money was? ☐

2 Right or wrong?

A. Sarah **said that she** was coming soon. ☐
B. Sarah **said she** was coming soon. ☐

3 Which sentence ending(s) is/are right?

I knew my English ... .

A. ... is getting better. ☐
B. ... was getting better. ☐
C. ....got better. ☐

▶

4 Which of these verb forms can fill the gap correctly?
I found out that Peter .... in Paris ten years ago.

A. grows up ☐
B. has grown up ☐
C. had grown up ☐

5 Which of these verbs can fill the gap correctly?
She said she .... see us later.

A. may ☐
B. might ☐
C. will ☐

6 Which word(s) can end the sentence: A, B or both?
I was talking to Bill on Saturday. He was a bit upset; he said he'd had an accident ...

A. ... yesterday. ☐
B. ... the day before. ☐

7 Is this sentence right or wrong? If it's wrong, correct it.

I told the police I was British. ___

....

8 Which word(s) can end the sentence correctly?
I asked where ...

A. ... Alice is. ☐
B. ... is Alice. ☐
C. ... Alice was. ☐
D. ... was Alice. ☐

9 Right or wrong?

A. I'm not sure if I **see** her tomorrow. ___
B. I'm not sure if **I'll see** her tomorrow. ___

22 relatives

1 Right R or wrong W?

A. I found the key I had lost. ___
B. This is the key opens the front door. ___

2 *Who, which* or both?

A. What's the name of the tall man .... just came in?
B. It's a book .... will interest children of all ages.
C. The course is for people .... are scared of flying. ▶

3 A, B or both?

Who's the girl .... with your brother?

A. who's dancing ☐
B. dancing ☐

4 Right or wrong?

A. I like people **who** smile a lot. ___
B. I like people **that** smile a lot. ___
C. I forget most of the films **which** I see. ___
D. I forget most of the films **that** I see. ___

5 Is this sentence right or wrong? If it's wrong, correct it.

Here's an article which it might interest you. ___

....

6 Do you need to add punctuation to these sentences: yes Y or no N? If you need to add punctuation, correct the sentences.

A. The man who cleans my windows has hurt his back. ___

....

B. Fred who cleans my windows has hurt his back. ___

....

7 *What, that,* or both?

A. .... she said made me very angry.
B. The things .... she said made me very angry.
C. Why can't you give me .... I need?
D. The only thing .... keeps me awake at night is coffee.

8 Which of the sentence endings is/are right?

I do a lot of walking, ...

A. ... **and this** keeps me fit. ☐
B. ... **which** keeps me fit. ☐
C. ... **what** keeps me fit. ☐

9 Right or wrong?

A. The teacher **I like best** is my English teacher. ___
B. The teacher **who I like best** is my English teacher. ___
C. The teacher **whom I like best** is my English teacher. ___

23 special sentence structures

1 Which sounds more natural: A or B?

A. To book in advance is important. ☐
B. It is important to book in advance. ☐

2 Choose the right option for each sentence.

A. It's worth .... (*to go, going*) to Wales if you have the time.
B. It's no use .... (*to try, trying*) to explain – I'm not interested.
C. It surprised me your not .... (*to remember, remembering*) my name.

3 Right R or wrong W?

A. I took three hours to get home last night. ☐
B. The journey took me three hours. ☐
C. This house took six weeks to clean. ☐
D. It took six weeks to clean. ☐
E. It took us six weeks before we got the house clean. ☐

4 ~ It was Peter that my aunt took to London yesterday, not Lucy.
Which of these questions does this answer?

A. Did your aunt take Lucy to London yesterday? ☐
B. Did Lucy take your aunt to London yesterday? ☐

5 Which of these exclamations is/are correct?

A. Here comes Freddy! ☐
B. Here Freddy comes! ☐
C. Here comes she! ☐
D. Here she comes! ☐
E. Off go we! ☐
F. Off we go! ☐

6 Which of these sentences from novels is/are normally correct?

A. 'What do you mean?' **asked Henry.** ☐
B. 'What do you mean?' **Henry asked.** ☐
C. 'What do you mean?' **he asked.** ☐
D. 'What do you mean?' **asked he.** ☐

7 In which sentence(s) can the words in italics be left out?

A. These men and ***these*** women are heroes. ☐
B. She was poor but ***she was*** honest. ☐
C. The food is ready and the drinks ***are ready***. ☐
D. You can get here by car, ***by*** bus, or ***by*** train. ☐

▶

8 Right or wrong?

A. **Who** influenced me most as a child was my grandfather. ☐

B. My grandfather was **the person who** influenced me most as a child. ☐

9 Fill in the two missing words in each sentence.

A. The .... we always met was the café in the park.

B. The .... we always met was Tuesday.

C. The .... we met was to play chess.

10 Which option(s) can begin the sentence?

... I remember was a terrible pain in my head.

A. All ... ☐

B. The first thing ... ☐

C. The only thing ... ☐

24 spoken grammar

1 Right R or wrong W?

A. You're the new secretary, aren't you? ☐

B. Are you the new secretary, aren't you? ☐

C. You're not the new secretary, are you? ☐

2 Which of these question tags is/are used correctly?

A. Sally can speak French, **can't she?** ☐

B. You like oysters, **don't you?** ☐

C. You wouldn't like a puppy, **wouldn't you?** ☐

D. Harry gave you a cheque, **didn't he?** ☐

E. She doesn't smoke, **doesn't she?** ☐

3 Choose the right question tag.

A. They can all swim, ... (*can't they, don't they*)?

B. They all speak German, ... (*can't they, don't they*)?

C. You've brought the map, ... (*didn't you, haven't you*)?

D. He's coming next month, ... (*isn't he, doesn't he*)?

E. He comes every month, ... (*isn't he, doesn't he*)?

F. You wanted to come with us, ... (*didn't you, wouldn't you*)?

4 Right or wrong?

A. You never say what you're thinking, don't you? ☐

B. He could never refuse a drink, couldn't he? ☐

▶

5 Normal N, formal F or wrong W?

They promised to repay us within six months, …

A. … did they not? ____
B. … did not they? ____
C. … didn't they? ____

6 Turn these questions into statements with question tags, e.g.

Are you Spanish? → You're Spanish, aren't you?

A. Do you know my sister? ______

B. Is the office on the first floor? ______

C. Do you like chocolate cake? ______

D. Would you like some more tea? ______

E. Did you speak to my boss at the meeting? ______

F. Can you ride a bicycle? ______

G. Will you come again next week? ______

7 Kevin the teenager is talking to his grandmother. Change his Yes/No answers to proper short answers, e.g.

Are you enjoying school, Kevin? ~ Yes. → Yes, I am.

A. Do you like your teachers? ~ Yes. ______
B. Are your teachers nice to you? ~ Yes. ______
C. Have you decided what you want to do once you've left school? ~ No. ______
D. Would you like to go to university? ~ No. ______
E. Will you go to university if your parents want you to? ~ No. ______

8 Answer these questions with short answers (not just *Yes/No*) that are true for you.

A. Can you play the piano? ______
B. Do you do some exercise every day? ______
C. Would you like to take more holidays? ______
D. Have you got a bicycle? ______
E. Did you do a lot of sport at primary school? ______
F. Will you retire at 60? ______

25 topic-related language

1 Right R or wrong W?

A. He's thirty. ___
B. He's thirty years. ___
C. He's thirty years old. ___
D. He's thirty years of age. ___

2 Which of these sentences is/are right?

A. **When I was your age** I had a job. ☐
B. **When I was at your age** I had a job. ☐
C. **At your age** I had a job. ☐
D. He could read **at the age** of three. ☐
E. He could read **in the age** of three. ☐

3 9 July → 9th July

Write these dates in the form above.

A. 3 August ....
B. 13 June ....
C. 22 September ....
D. 21 November ....

4 Write the full form of the date *6/9/05* ...

A. ... in Britain: ....
B. ... in the USA: ....

5 Which of these ways of getting someone's attention is/are normal?

A. Excuse me. ☐
B. Excuse me, Mr. ☐
C. Excuse me, Mrs. ☐
D. Excuse me, sir. ☐
E. Excuse me, madam. ☐

▶

6 Complete the table.

	Country/ region	Adjective	Person	Population
	Brazil	Brazilian	a Brazilian	the Brazilians
A.	Europe			
B.	Italy			
C.	England			
D.	Portugal			
E.	France			
F.	China			
G.	Spain			
H.	Britain			

7 Which of these ways of identifying yourself on the phone is/are normal?

Could I speak to Jane Horrabin?

A. ~ **I'm** Jane Horrabin. ☐
B. ~ **This is** Jane Horrabin. ☐
C. ~ **This is** Jane Horrabin **speaking**. ☐
D. ~ **Speaking**. ☐

8 Choose the right option(s) for each of these telephoning expressions (in British English). Sometimes more than one option is possible.

A. I'm afraid she's not .... (*in, there, present*) at the moment.
B. Can I .... (*give, leave, pass*) a message?
C. Can I .... (*receive, get, take*) a message?
D. I'll .... (*ring back, call back, call again*) later.
E. Could you ask her to .... (*call back me, call me back*) .... (*at, on, to*) 2228 1234?

9 Are these ways of saying the time right or wrong (in British English)?

08:50

A. eight fifty ____
B. ten to nine ____
C. eight fifty a.m. ____

4.30

D. four thirty ____
E. half four ____
F. half past four ____
G. half past four o'clock ____

26 spelling, contractions and punctuation

1 Which of these should normally have capital letters?

A. the **e**arth ☐
B. the **s**un ☐
C. the **m**oon ☐
D. **m**ars ☐
E. on **t**uesday ☐
F. at **e**aster ☐
G. next **s**ummer ☐

2 Which of these are right?

A. He's a **H**indu. ☐
B. She's **j**ewish. ☐
C. He's **r**ussian. ☐
D. He studies **j**apanese **h**istory. ☐
E. He studies **J**apanese **h**istory. ☐
F. He studies **J**apanese **H**istory. ☐

3 Change these words to adverbs, e.g.

right → rightly .

A. real ....
B. complete ....
C. true ....
D. whole ....
E. full ....
F. happy ....
I. idle ....
J. able ....

4 Insert hyphens (-) in this sentence where they are needed.

My sister in law has agreed to baby sit so that we can go to next week's Scotland France rugby match. ▶

5 Is the spelling of the highlighted word right R or wrong W? If it's wrong, correct it.

A. I was **hoping** for a pay rise.

⎣__⎦ ....

B. We found a **shadey** beach, five minutes' walk from the hotel.

⎣__⎦ ....

C. We've had a most **agreeable** evening.

⎣__⎦ ....

D. She was late and I was **begining** to worry.

⎣__⎦ ....

E. Thanks for inviting me, but I hadn't **planned** to go out tonight.

⎣__⎦ ....

6 Which spelling(s) is/are right: the first, the second or both?

A. excitment ☐ excitement ☐
B. definitly ☐ definitely ☐
C. argument ☐ arguement ☐

7 Right or wrong?

A. Have you **layed** the table yet? ⎣__⎦
B. She **played** the piano for us. ⎣__⎦
C. I **payed** the electricity bill yesterday. ⎣__⎦

8 Which of these is/are a spelling rule learnt by English-speaking children?

A. 'i before e, except after c.' ☐
B. 'i before e, except after g.' ☐
C. 'i before e, except after t.' ☐

9 Cross out the letter(s) that is/are not normally pronounced, e.g.

ASP~~I~~RIN DAU~~GH~~TER

A. BUSINESS
B. CHOCOLATE
C. DIFFERENT
D. MARRIAGE
E. RESTAURANT
F. COMFORTABLE
G. INTERESTING
H. USUALLY

▶

10 In which words are the highlighted letters NOT normally pronounced?

A. CLIM**B** ☐
B. CUCUM**B**ER ☐
C. MUS**C**LE ☐
D. MUS**C**ULAR ☐
E. **H**ONEST ☐
F. **H**ORRIBLE ☐
G. **H**ONOUR ☐
H. **W**RITE ☐
I. **W**RONG ☐
J. **W**HO ☐

11 In which THREE words is *ea* pronounced differently from the others?

A. H**EA**D ☐
B. ALR**EA**DY ☐
C. PL**EA**SURE ☐
D. BR**EA**K ☐
E. THR**EA**T ☐
F. SW**EA**TER ☐
G. W**EA**THER ☐
H. GR**EA**T ☐
I. ST**EA**K ☐
J. M**EA**NT ☐

12 And in which THREE words is *o* pronounced differently from the others?

A. T**O** ☐
B. BR**O**THER ☐
C. C**O**ME ☐
D. L**O**SE ☐
E. M**O**NEY ☐
F. N**O**NE ☐
G. PR**O**VE ☐
H. T**O**NGUE ☐
I. W**O**N ☐
J. AB**O**VE ☐

13 Right or wrong?

A. **She hadn't** been there for more than five minutes before he arrived. ___
B. **She'd not** been there for more than five minutes before he arrived. ___
C. Take a seat – **I won't** be long. ___
D. Take a seat – **I'll not** be long. ___
E. I'm afraid **she isn't** coming. ___
F. I'm afraid **she's not** coming. ___

14 Which of the equivalent forms is/are possible?

it's

A. it is ☐
B. it has ☐
C. it was ☐

you'd

D. you did ☐
E. you had ☐
F. you would ☐

▶

15 Right or wrong (in standard British English)?

A. I'm late, **amn't I**? ⎵

B. He's late, **isn't he**? ⎵

C. They're late, **aren't they**? ⎵

16 What goes here ▒ : comma (,) or no comma (leave blank)?

A. It is quite natural ▒ that you should want to see your father.

B. Your father ▒ however ▒ did not agree.

C. The driver ▒ in the Ferrari ▒ was cornering superbly.

D. What we need most of all ▒ is more time.

E. Everybody realised ▒ that I was a foreigner.

17 Are the apostrophes (') right or wrong? If they're wrong, correct the word they're used in.

A. The money is your**'**s. ⎵ ....

B. The cat has**'**nt had it**'**s food yet. ⎵ ....

C. Who**'**s house did she stay in? ⎵ ....

27 words (1): similar words

1 *First* or *at first*?

A. .... beat the eggs. Then pour in the milk.

B. They were very happy ....; then they started having problems.

C. We lived there when we were .... married.

D. .... I was very lonely, but I soon made lots of friends.

2 *Beside, besides* or both?

A. .... chemistry, I also have to study biology and physics.

B. Come and sit down .... me.

C. It's too late to go out now; .... it's starting to rain.

3 Which of these sentences is/are right?

A. Be careful when you're crossing the road. ☐

B. Take care when you're crossing the road. ☐

C. Take care of crossing the road. ☐

4 He doesn't .... other people's opinions.

Which is the right option: A, B, C or D?

A. care ☐

B. care about ☐

C. care for ☐

D. take care of ☐

▶

5 ***Cloth, clothes,* or *clothing*?**

A. This dress is the only piece of ________ that I bought in this year's sale.

B. It's made from a very expensive ________ that you can only get in India.

6 ***Experience, experiences* or *experiments*?**

A. We did some interesting ________ in the science lesson.

B. I had a bad ________ with my first skiing lesson.

C. Since I moved abroad, I've had lots of different ________ .

D. If you want to get this promotion, you need lots more ________ .

7 **Right R or wrong W?**

A. London is **farther** from Edinburgh than it is from Paris. ☐

B. London is **further** from Edinburgh than it is from Paris. ☐

C. For **farther** information, please call or email me. ☐

D. For **further** information, please call or email me. ☐

8 ***Male* or *masculine*?**

A. A ________ sheep is called a ram.

B. I thought she was a man when she phoned me; she has a very ________ voice.

C. The word 'courage' is ________ gender in French: it's *le courage.*

D. *[in a form]*- **Name:** Jim Murphy; **Age:** 42; **Sex:** ________ **Nationality**: Irish.

9 ***Fun, funny* or both?**

A. He was wearing ________ clothes; he looked like a clown.

B. The party was really ________ . Thanks for inviting me.

C. My fish tastes a bit ________ . Does yours?

D. That was such a ________ holiday; let's do it again next year.

10 ***Older, elder* or both?**

A. My ________ brother has just got married.

B. My brother is three years ________ than me. ▶

11 Right or wrong? If any are wrong, correct them.

A. **Its** raining again. ⎣__⎦ ....
B. Have you seen my camera? **It's** disappeared. ⎣__⎦ ....
C. The dog has lost **it's** ball. Can you see it? ⎣__⎦ ....
D. Every country has **its'** traditions. ⎣__⎦ ....

12 Is this sentence right or wrong? If it's wrong, correct it.

I must be **loosing** weight: my clothes feel very **loose**. ⎣__⎦

....

13 Which expression(s) can end the sentence correctly?
All the students went on strike…

A. ... but no teachers joined in. ☐
B. ... but not the teachers joined in. ☐
C. ... but no the teachers. ☐
D. ... but not the teachers. ☐

14 Which is/are correct? A, B or both?

A. I've got no Tuesdays free this term. ☐
B. I haven't got any Tuesdays free this term. ☐

15 ~ €2000 – it's a great price!
Which question(s) does this answer?

A. How much did you win in the lottery? ☐
B. How much did you earn last month? ☐
C. How much did you pay for your last holiday? ☐

28 words (2): other confusable words

1 *Begin, start* or both?

A. Did you .... playing the piano when you were a small child?
B. We will .... the conference with a message from the president.
C. I think we ought to .... at six, while the roads are still empty.

2 *Lend, borrow* or both?

Can I .... your bicycle to go to the shops? ▶

3 Right R or wrong W?

A. I borrowed some money from my brother and now I can't pay it back. ⎣__⎦
B. I borrowed my brother some money and now I can't pay it back. ⎣__⎦
C. I lent my coat to Steve and I never saw it again. ⎣__⎦
D. I lent Steve my coat and I never saw it again. ⎣__⎦

4 *Bring, take* or both (in British English)?

A. This is a great party. It was nice of you to .... me here.
B. Let's have one more drink, and then I'll .... you home.

5 *Broad, wide* or both?

A. The car is too .... for the garage.
B. The river is about a kilometre ....
C. Everyone loves pandas: it's because of their beautiful .... eyes.
D. We've reached .... agreement on all the most important issues.

6 *Close(d), shut*, or both?

A. I .... the door and sat down.
B. I hadn't realised that the shop .... at five.
C. *[Dentist to patient]* Now .... your mouth, please.
D. The dog wouldn't stop barking, so we .... him out of the house.
E. The chairman .... the meeting with a vote of thanks.
F. The railway line was .... because there were leaves on the track.

7 *Come* or *go*? Right or wrong?

A. Maria, would you come here please? ~ OK, I'm **going**. ⎣__⎦
B. Let's **go** and visit your parents. ⎣__⎦
C. Can I **come** and see you soon? ⎣__⎦

▶

8 *Do* or *make*?

A. I'm not going to .... any work today.
B. I think I'll .... a cake for Jake's party.
C. We need to .... a plan, in case we have problems tomorrow.
D. Can you .... the shopping, please?
E. Can you .... me a big favour?
F. My new boss finds it hard to .... a decision.
G. You really need to .... an effort!
H. You really need to .... your best!

9 Which is better: *end/ended* or *finish/finished*?

A. The Second World War .... in 1945.
B. The footpath .... at the farmhouse.
C. Should I .... this letter with 'Yours faithfully' or 'Yours sincerely'?
D. Yesterday I .... working in the garden when it got dark.

10 *Fit* or *suit*?

A. These shoes don't .... me: have you got a larger size?
B. Have you got the same jacket in grey? Brown doesn't .... me.
C. When can we meet next week? ~ Does Tuesday .... you?

11 *Forget, leave* or both?

Where's your umbrella? Did you .... it at home?

12 Fill in the gaps using *hear* or *listen to* (in the correct form).

A. I once .... Frank Sinatra singing live.
B. Have you .... the news? There's been a terrible accident.
C. When you phoned, I was .... the news on the radio.
D. I .... them talking, but I wasn't really .... their conversation.

13 *Here* or *there*?

A. Who's that? ~ It's Sarah ....
B. Hello, Sarah. Is Tom .... ? ~ No, I'm sorry he isn't .... ▶

14 *High, tall* or *long*?

A. How .... are you?
B. There's a beautiful .... tree in the garden.
C. Could you pass me a tin of peaches, please? That shelf is too .... for me.
D. Alex has got beautiful .... legs.

15 Right or wrong?

A. **How's** Adrian? ~ He's quiet and a bit shy. ☐
B. **What's** Adrian **like**? ~ He's quiet and a bit shy. ☐
C. **How was** the film? ~ Very funny and well acted, but a bit too long. ☐
D. **What was** the film **like**? ~ Very funny and well acted, but a bit too long. ☐

16 *Opportunity, possibility* or both?

I have the .... to go to Denmark this year.

17 *Play, game* or both?

A. Chess is a very slow ....
B. Children learn a great deal through ....

18 *Small* or *little*?

A. Two .... whiskies, please.
B. He wears a ring on his .... finger.
C. He's too .... to play in goal.
D. You're a very naughty .... girl!
E. The baby looked so .... and helpless.

19 *Soon, early* or *quickly*? (More than one might be possible.)

A. We usually go on holiday .... in the year.
B. I usually get up .... – at about 6.30 a.m.
C. Best wishes for a/an .... recovery.
D. I hope you can do the repair .... – I really need the car.
E. He did the repair much too .... and it's still not working.

►

20 Complete each sentence with one of these words: *travel, travels, journey, trip, voyage*. Use each word just once.

A. My aunt loves travelling by boat. She's just completed a three-month .... to south-east Asia.

B. How was your .... here? ~ Terrible. My train broke down twice.

C. My main interests are music and ....

D. The school is organizing a skiing .... to the Alps.

E. He told me all about his exciting .... in rural Africa.

21 Which sounds better: *far* or *a long way*?

A. You'd better leave now. The station is .... from here.

B. The bank is not .... from here.

C. We walked .... to the beach.

22 *Say* or *tell*? Right or wrong?

A. 'Look, what's your problem?' I **told** her. ☐

B. I just don't think she's **saying** the truth. ☐

C. He's seven years old and he can't **tell** the time. ☐

D. She **told** that she had lost all her money. ☐

E. Can you **say** me where to find a good cheap restaurant? ☐

23 *Such* or *so*?

A. He's .... silly!

B. They're .... idiots!

C. They're .... a nice couple!

D. It was .... good milk that we couldn't stop drinking it.

E. Why do you speak .... slowly?

24 *Beat, win* or both?

My boyfriend .... me at tennis last Saturday.

25 Which is correct?

A. Scotland is in the north of England. ☐

B. Scotland is in the west of England. ☐

C. Scotland is not in England. ☐

29 words (3): other vocabulary problems

1 What does *actually* mean here?
We're meeting him at the office. ~ **Actually**, we're meeting him at his hotel.

A. In fact, we're not meeting him at the office but at his hotel. ☐
B. We're meeting him at his hotel now and at his office later. ☐

2 Which of these sentences is/are right?

A. I'm **quite fitter** since I started jogging. ☐
B. I'm **completely fitter** since I started jogging. ☐
C. Don't start work until you're **quite better**. ☐
D. Don't start work until you're **completely better**. ☐

3 *Better, rather* or both?

I'd like a coffee – or ...., a cappuccino.

4 Alice **called** this morning.
What does this mean?

A. She telephoned. ☐
B. She visited. ☐
C. We can't tell from this sentence alone. ☐

5 Right R or wrong W? Replace the verb *control* with another verb, if you think it's being used incorrectly.

A. The crowd was too big for the police to **control**. ____

....

B. The police were **controlling** everyone's papers. ____

....

C. I found the car difficult to **control** at high speeds. ____

....

D. I took the car to the garage and asked them to **control** the steering. ____

....

6 Right or wrong?

A. My parents live in **a nice country** near Oxford. ____
B. Would you rather live in **a town** or **a country**? ____
C. Which **countries** have you worked in? ____

7 Right or wrong?

A. She looks good in **a red dress.** ____
B. He looks good in **an evening dress**. ____

▶

8 Choose the right option for each sentence.

A. Could you .... (*dress, get dressed*) the children for me?
B. .... (*Dress, Get dressed*) and come downstairs at once!
C. I .... (*dressed in, dressed with, put on*) a sweater, but it was so warm that I had to .... (*undress it, take it off*).

9 Is *enjoy* used rightly or wrongly here? If it's wrong, correct it.

A. Did you enjoy the party? ~ Yes, I **enjoyed** very much. ⎵

....

B. I don't **enjoy to look after** small children. ⎵

....

C. We're going to Paris for the weekend.~ **Enjoy yourself**! ⎵

....

10 Choose the right option(s). More than one may be possible.

A. Everybody helped with the packing – .... (*even, also*) the kids.
B. .... (*Even, Even if*) I become a millionaire, I'll still be a socialist.
C. .... (*Even though, Even although*) I didn't know anybody at the party, I had a nice time.
D. I'll do it, ... (*if, even if*) it kills me.
E. He seems nice. .... (*Even so, Even though*), I don't trust him.

11 He left her ten years ago, but **even now** she still loves him.
What does this sentence mean?

A. She still loves him just as much as before. ☐
B. In spite of everything that has happened, she still loves him. ☐

12 Which is the right beginning for this sentence: A or B?
... **eventually** I'll go to America.

A. It'll take a long time and I'll need to save my money, but ... ☐
B. I don't know what I'm going to do next year; ... ☐

13 Which of these is/are right?

A. I explained her my problem. ☐
B. I explained my problem to her. ☐
C. Can you suggest us a restaurant? ☐
D. Can you suggest a restaurant to us? ☐

▶

14 Right or wrong?

A. Her uncle **suggested her to get** a job in a bank. ⌴
B. Her uncle **suggested that she should get** a job in a bank. ⌴
C. Her uncle **suggested getting** a job in a bank. ⌴

15 Right or wrong? If it's wrong, correct it.

A. I'm **getting** tired – let's go home. ⌴

....

B. Wayne's **getting** a lovely kid. ⌴

....

16 Rewrite these sentences by replacing the highlighted verb with an equivalent, beginning with *get*, e.g.

You can't **make** him **leave** his bed in the morning.

→ You can't **get** him **out** of bed in the morning.

A. **Make** the dog **leave** the bedroom.

....

B. **Remove** your papers from my desk.

....

C. Will this bus **return** us to the airport?

....

17 Are these sentences right or wrong? If they're wrong, correct them.

A. I can't **get** the children **going** to bed. ⌴

....

B. Once we **got** the heater **going**, the car started to warm up. ⌴

....

18 Right or wrong?

A. I **got** my shoes cleaned. ⌴
B. I **got** my shoes stolen. ⌴

19 Which of these is/are right?

A. Is anybody **home**? ☐
B. Is anybody **at home**? ☐
C. Is anybody **at the home**? ☐
D. I'm going **home**. ☐
E. I'm going **at home**. ☐
F. I'm going **to home**. ☐

►

20 Right or wrong?

A. Ann enjoys **life.** ☐
B. Ann enjoys **city life.** ☐
C. My grandparents had **hard life.** ☐
D. My mother's parents lived **interesting lives.** ☐

21 Which of these is/are right?

A. I can't **make** the washing machine **work.** ☐
B. I can't **make work** the washing machine. ☐
C. I can't **make to work** the washing machine. ☐
D. I can't **make working** the washing machine. ☐
E. The rain **made wet** the grass. ☐
F. The rain **made** the grass **wet.** ☐
G. The rain **made** the grass **be wet.** ☐

22 Which of these is/are right?

A. She **married** a builder. ☐
B. She **married with** a builder. ☐
C. She **got married with** a builder. ☐
D. She **got married to** a builder. ☐

23 Right or wrong? Replace the word *open* with another word, if you think it's being used incorrectly.

A. I can't **open** this shoelace. ☐ ....
B. Are the banks **open** today? ☐ ....
C. Could you **open** the radio – I want to hear the news. ☐ ....
D. Who left the taps **open**? ☐ ....

24 Which expression(s) can end the sentence correctly?

It's nice if she can have ...

A. ... an own room. ☐
B. ... her own room. ☐
C. ... a room of her own. ☐

25 Which of these is/are right?

A. Give me **same again**, please. ☐
B. Give me **the same again**, please. ☐
C. You've had **the same idea as me.** ☐
D. You've had **my same idea.** ☐
E. Her hair's the same colour **as** her mother's. ☐
F. Her hair's the same colour **like** her mother's. ☐

▶

26 ***Such* or *so*?**

A. They're .... fools!
B. He's .... babyish!
C. It was .... good milk that we couldn't stop drinking it.
D. The milk was .... good that we couldn't stop drinking it.
E. We've got .... little time left.
F. I've never met .... a nice person.

27 Which expression(s) can complete the sentence correctly?
I'm glad you're feeling ...

A. ... so better. ☐
B. ... so much better. ☐
C. ... such much better. ☐

28 What does this sentence mean?
I'm **sympathetic** towards the strikers.

A. I agree with the strikers' aims. ☐
B. I behave kindly towards the strikers. ☐

Adv

LEVEL 2

Advanced

LEVEL 2 Advanced

1 present and future verbs

1 Which expression(s) can normally end the sentence correctly?
House prices go up ...

A. ... every year. ☐
B. ... again. ☐
C. ... by 2% this year. ☐
D. ... when there are not enough new houses. ☐

2 Right R or wrong W?

A. Here **comes** our train. ___
B. Here **is coming** our train. ___

3 Which of these is more usual: A or B?

A. **It says** in the instructions that you need two 9-volt batteries. ☐
B. **It's saying** in the instructions that you need two 9-volt batteries. ☐

4 Which question is the more likely response: A or B?
Jake's just phoned in to say he's ill.

A. ~ So **who's going to teach** his class this afternoon? ☐
B. ~ So **who's teaching** his class this afternoon? ☐

5 Which sounds more polite: A or B?

A. **I hope** you can help me. ☐
B. **I'm hoping** you can help me. ☐

6 Which is more normal: A or B?

A. **I promise** never to smoke again. ☐
B. **I'm promising** never to smoke again. ☐

7 Which is the best way to end the sentence: A, B or C?
I'm seeing my boss tomorrow and ...

A. ... **I'm complaining** about this year's pay rise. ☐
B. ... **I'm going to complain** about this year's pay rise. ☐
C. ... **I will complain** about this year's pay rise. ☐

8 Right or wrong?

A. **It's snowing** before long. ___
B. **It's going to snow** before long. ___
C. **It'll be snowing** before long. ___

9 Right or wrong?

A. **You're going to take** that medicine, whether you like it or not! ___
B. **You're taking** that medicine, whether you like it or not! ___

▶

10 Which of these sports commentaries uses the present tense correctly: A, B or both?

A. 'Smith **passes** to Devaney; Harris **intercepts**. Harris **passes back** to Simms and Simms **shoots**!' ☐

B. 'Oxford **are pulling** ahead of Cambridge. They'**re rowing** steadily. Cambridge **are looking** a bit disorganised.' ☐

11 Right or wrong?

A. Don't phone them now – **they're having** dinner. ___

B. Don't phone them now – **they'll be having** dinner. ___

12 Which is the best way to end the sentence: A, B or C?

This time tomorrow ...

A. ... **I'm lying** on the beach. ☐

B. ... **I'll lie** on the beach. ☐

C. ... **I'll be lying** on the beach. ☐

13 Which expression(s) can end the sentence correctly?

The builders say they **will have** finished the roof ...

A. ... by Tuesday. ☐

B. ... by the end of the week. ☐

C. ... as soon as they can. ☐

D. ... without any more delays. ☐

2 past and perfect verbs

1 Which expression(s) can end the sentence correctly?

She realised ...

A. ... **she had not** locked the front door. ☐

B. ... **she hadn't** locked the front door. ☐

C. ... **she'd not** locked the front door. ☐

2 Right R or wrong W?

A. When I was a child, **we made** our own amusements. ___

B. When I was a child, **we played** outside every day. ___

C. At the time when it happened, **I was travelling** to New York a lot. ___

3 Which of these sentences is/are correct?

A. I lived in London for three years while I was a student. ☐

B. When I got home, water was coming through the ceiling. ☐

C. It happened while I stayed with my parents last weekend. ☐

▶

4 Which of these questions is/are correct (in British English)?

A. Are you finished yet? ☐
B. Have you finished yet? ☐
C. Did you finish yet? ☐

5 Look at these questions:

i. How long **are you** here for?
ii. How long **were you** here for?
iii. How long **have you been** here for?

Which of these statements is true: A, B or C?

A. They all mean the same. ☐
B. Two of them mean the same. ☐
C. They all mean something different. ☐

6 Right or wrong?

A. How long **are you** studying English? ___
B. How long **have you been** studying English? ___

7 Which of these structures is/are normally correct?

A. I've met her before she started working here. ☐
B. I'm sure we've met before. ☐
C. I haven't been abroad recently. ☐
D. I've bought a new car recently. ☐
E. She's never said 'sorry' in her life. ☐
F. I never said 'sorry' when I had the chance. ☐

8 Right or wrong?

A. When I was a child, **we always went swimming** on Saturdays in the summer. ___
B. Her mother **was always arranging** little surprise picnics and outings. ___

9 Is this sentence right or wrong? If it's wrong, correct it.

Yesterday's maths exam was very hard, but I think we've studied enough to pass it. ___

....

10 Right or wrong?

A. It **was raining** all day. I'm tired of it! ___
B. It**'s rained** all day. I'm tired of it! ___
C. It**'s been raining** all day. I'm tired of it! ___

▶

11 Which of the replies can be used correctly?
You look hot.

A. ~ Yes, I ran here. ☐
B. ~ Yes, I've run. ☐
C. ~ Yes, I've been running. ☐

12 Which of the replies can be used correctly?
You look tired.

A. ~ I woke up all night. ☐
B. ~ I've woken up all night. ☐
C. ~ I've been waking up all night. ☐

13 Which sentence(s) can follow this one?
I need to change my TV.

A. It **didn't work** very well recently. ☐
B. It **hasn't worked** very well recently. ☐
C. It **hasn't been working** very well recently. ☐

14 Right or wrong?

A. That man **has been standing** at the bus stop all day. ___
B. For 900 years the castle **has stood** on the hill above the village. ___

15 Which sentence(s) can follow this one?
I've been planting rose bushes all morning.

A. Look at all the bushes **I was planting**! ☐
B. Look at all the bushes **I've planted**! ☐
C. Look at all the bushes **I've been planting**! ☐

16 Which expression(s) can end the sentence correctly?
It's the fifth time ...

A. ... **you ask** the same question. ☐
B. ... **you are asking** the same question. ☐
C. ... **you asked** the same question. ☐
D. ... **you've asked** the same question. ☐

17 Which expression(s) can end the sentence correctly?
It's been raining ...

A. ... for the last few days. ☐
B. ... since last week. ☐
C. ... in September. ☐
D. ... from seven in the morning till lunchtime. ☐
E. ... recently. ☐
F. ... this week. ☐
G. ... last week. ☐

▶

18 Right or wrong?

A. My legs were stiff because I **had been standing** still for a long time. ⎵

B. The tree that blew down **had stood** there for 300 years. ⎵

3 auxiliary verbs

1 Right R or wrong W?

I felt nervous because ...

A. ... I was soon **going to** leave home for the first time. ⎵

B. ... I was soon **to** leave home for the first time. ⎵

2 What does this sentence mean?

I was to have started work last week.

A. I was supposed to start work before last week. ☐

B. I was supposed to start work last week, but I didn't. ☐

3 Which verb form(s) can complete the sentence correctly?

If we .... by lunchtime, we had better hurry.

A. get there ☐

B. will get there ☐

C. would get there ☐

D. are to get there ☐

4 Which of these would you see on a medicine bottle?

A. **Take** three times a day after meals. ☐

B. **To take** three times a day after meals. ☐

C. **To be taken** three times a day after meals. ☐

5 I'm ready to see Mr Smith now. ...

Which of these can follow the sentence above?

A. ... Have him come in, please. ☐

B. ... Have him coming in, please. ☐

C. ... Have him to come in, please. ☐

D. ... Make him come in, please. ☐

6 Are these replies right or wrong (in British English)?

Close the door!

A. ~ I have. ⎵

B. ~ I've done. ⎵

C. ~ I have done. ⎵

D. ~ I have closed it. ⎵

▶

Adv

7 Which expression(s) can complete the sentence correctly?
He .... all through the meeting.

A. made us laugh ☐
B. made us laughing ☐
C. had us laugh ☐
D. had us laughing ☐

8 Is this sentence right or wrong? If it's wrong, correct it.
I had a very strange thing happen to me when I was fourteen. ___

....

9 What does this sentence mean?
I won't have you telling me what to do.

A. I won't ask you to tell me what to do. ☐
B. I won't let you tell me what to do. ☐

4 modal verbs (1): *can, could, may, might*

1 Right R or wrong W?

A. Can I ask you something? ~ Yes, of course **you can**. ___
B. Could I ask you something? ~ Yes, of course **you could**. ___

2 Right or wrong? Correct any wrong sentences.

A. When I was younger, I **could** run 10 km in 40 minutes. ___

....

B. I **could** run 10 km yesterday in under an hour. ___

....

C. I managed to find the street, but I **wasn't able to** find her house. ___

....

D. I managed to find the street, but I **couldn't** find her house. ___

....

3 Right or wrong? Correct any wrong sentences.

A. When I was a child, I **could** watch TV whenever I wanted to. ___

....

B. Yesterday evening, Peter **could** watch TV for an hour. ___

....

C. Peter **couldn't** watch TV yesterday because he was naughty. ___

....

▶

4 Which of these modal verb forms is/are used correctly?

A. **Could** I have another cup of tea, please? ☐
B. **May** I have another cup of tea, please? ☐
C. **Might** I have another cup of tea, please? ☐
D. **I wonder if I might** have another cup of tea, please. ☐

5 Which modal verb form(s) can complete the reply?
Who sent these flowers? ~ I'm not sure. It .... your mother.

A. **could** have been ☐
B. **might** have been ☐
C. **may** have been ☐

6 You **could** ask before you borrow my car.
Is this probably...

A. ... a suggestion? ☐
B. ... a request? ☐
C. ... a criticism? ☐

7 *Could know* or *could tell*?

A. I .... what she wanted.
B. You .... he was Irish from his accent.

8 *Wouldn't* or *couldn't*?
I asked her to meet me tonight, but ...

A. ... she said she .... as she had a meeting.
B. ... she said she .... as she was still angry with me.

9 Is this sentence right or wrong? If it's wrong, correct it.
If you worked less hard, you **may** feel less tired. ⎵⎵⎵

....

10 Right or wrong?

A. I hope that the young couple **will** enjoy years of happiness. ⎵⎵⎵
B. I hope that the young couple **may** enjoy years of happiness. ⎵⎵⎵
C. I hope that the young couple **might** enjoy years of happiness. ⎵⎵⎵
D. **May** you both be very happy together! ⎵⎵⎵

11 Which expression(s) can end the sentence: A, B or both?
She **might have told me** she was going to stay out all night; ...

A. ... I really can't remember. ☐
B. ... I'm so angry with her. ☐

▶

12 Right or wrong?

A. He **can't have got** my message. ☐
B. He **couldn't have got** my message. ☐
C. He **may not have got** my message. ☐
D. He **might not have got** my message. ☐

13 Which of the sentences in Question 12 above mean(s) the same as *I'm sure he didn't get my message*? ☐

5 modal verbs (2): *will, would, used to, must, should, ought*

1 What does the writer of this letter mean?
Dear Sir – You **will recently have received** our new price list.

A. I think you received our new price list recently. ☐
B. I'm certain that you received our new price list recently. ☐

2 Right R **or wrong** W**?**

A. **What would you like** to drink? ☐
B. **What will you** drink? ☐
C. **Will you have** some more wine? ☐
D. **Won't you have** some more wine? ☐

3 Right or wrong?

A. **Will you** come this way, please? ☐
B. **Would you** come this way, please? ☐
C. Come this way, **would you**? ☐

4 Which replies can be used correctly?
We went on a cruise last month.

A. ~ That **must** have been nice. ☐
B. ~ That **should** have been nice. ☐
C. ~ That **can't** have been cheap. ☐

5 Which question tag(s) can end the sentence?
It must be nice to be so popular, ...

A. ... isn't it? ☐ B. ... can't it? ☐ C. ... mustn't it? ☐

6 Which expression(s) can end the sentence?
My doctor said that I ...

A. ... **had to** stop smoking. ☐
B. ... **must** stop smoking. ☐
C. ... **would have to** stop smoking. ☐

▶

7 Which verb form(s) can complete the sentence correctly?
She .... in the meeting, but she wasn't there.

A. should be ☐
B. should have been ☐
C. was supposed to be ☐

8 Right or wrong?

A. It **oughtn't** rain today. ___
B. We ought to leave now, **oughtn't we**? ___

9 Which two sentences mean the same?

A. You **must be** more careful. ☐
B. You **ought to be** more careful. ☐
C. You **should be** more careful. ☐

10 Which question is best if you're talking to a friend?

A. **Do you think we ought to** go now? ☐
B. **Ought we to** go now? ☐

11 Which modal verb can you use (instead of *ought*) to make the previous question less formal?

.... we go now?

12 Right or wrong?

A. You **always ought to have** your mobile phone with you. ___
B. You **ought always to have** your mobile phone with you. ___
C. You **ought not to forget** your phone when you go out. ___
D. You **ought to not forget** your phone when you go out. ___

13 Which is the strongest advice: A, B or C?

A. You **should** lose weight. ☐
B. You**'d better** lose weight. ☐
C. You **ought** to lose weight. ☐

14 What does this sentence mean?
Oh, it's you. I suppose **you'd better** come in.

A. I think it's better for you to come in than to stand outside. ☐
B. You can come in, but you aren't especially welcome. ☐

15 Right or wrong?

A. I **always used** to be afraid of dogs. ___
B. I **used always** to be afraid of dogs. ___

6 structures with infinitives

1 *To do, to be done* or both?

There's a lot of work ………… before we can take a break.

2 Right R or wrong W?

A. It's as easy to smile **as to frown.** ⎵
B. It's as easy to smile **as frown.** ⎵

3 Right or wrong?

A. She is the first woman **to win** a presidential election. ⎵
B. Is this the first time for you **to visit** this country? ⎵

4 Which of these infinitive verb form(s) is/are used correctly?

A. I have no wish **to cause** you problems. ☐
B. I hate the thought **to upset** you. ☐
C. I told her about my decision **to resign** immediately. ☐

5 *To repair, to repair it* or both?

A. I gave the man my watch ………… .
B. He told me that he didn't have time ………… straight away.

6 Right or wrong?

A. There wasn't **enough light** for me to see what I was doing. ⎵
B. There's **hardly enough room** to breathe in here. ⎵
C. There's **hardly room** to breathe in here. ⎵

7 I didn't know that Mary was John's **wife to be.** What does this sentence mean?

A. I didn't know that Mary was really John's wife. ☐
B. I didn't know that John was going to marry Mary. ☐

8 Right or wrong?

A. I meant to call her, but I **forgot to have called.** ⎵
B. She **was to have been** the next president, but she resigned suddenly. ⎵

9 Which sentence ending(s) is/are normal?

I moved house …

A. … **to be** nearer to my office. ☐
B. … **in order to be** nearer to my office. ☐
C. … **so as to be** nearer to my office. ☐
D. … **not to be** too far from my office. ☐
E. … **so as not to be** too far from my office. ☐

▶

10 Which sentence ending(s) is/are possible?
I left the door unlocked …

A. … for to get in. ☐
B. … for me to get in. ☐
C. … for Sarah to get in. ☐

11 They didn't keep John as their manager, which was a big mistake.
Fill in the four missing words to make a sentence with the same meaning.

It was a big mistake for ………… ………… ………… ………… John as their manager.

12 ***It, it was*** **or both?**

I thought ………………… strange **for her to be** out so late.

13 Which two of these sentences sound most natural?

A. **Your task was** to steal the secret formula, Mr Bond. ☐
B. To steal the secret formula **was your task**, Mr Bond. ☐
C. **It was your task** to steal the secret formula, Mr Bond. ☐

14 Which verb form(s) can complete the sentence correctly?
When he arrives ………………… very tired.

A. he'll probably be ☐
B. it's probable that he'll be ☐
C. it's probable for him to be ☐

15 What does this sentence mean?
I arrived at the shop **to find that** the door was locked.

A. The speaker couldn't remember whether she had locked the door of the shop, and went back to check. ☐
B. The speaker was expecting the door of the shop to be unlocked when she arrived, but it wasn't. ☐

16 To see them, you would think that they were best friends.
What does the speaker mean?

A. It's obvious that they really like each other. ☐
B. They don't really like each other, but are pretending that they do. ☐

Adv

7 *-ing* forms and past participles

1 Right R or wrong W?

A. She's worried about **not being** careful enough with her translation. ☐

B. She's worried about **not having been** careful enough with her translation. ☐

2 Right or wrong?

A. *THE SMOKING CIGARETTES IS STRICTLY PROHIBITED.* ☐

B. *THE SMOKING OF CIGARETTES IS STRICTLY PROHIBITED.* ☐

C. Sorry – there's no smoking here. ☐

3 *Him, his* or both?

A. I understood .... feeling angry with his daughter.

B. I saw .... getting angry with his daughter.

4 *Asking, to ask* or both?

I didn't think it worth .... him his opinion.

5 Which is more usual?

A. We're all shocked by his **resigning**. ☐

B. We're all shocked by his **resignation**. ☐

6 Which expression(s) can complete the sentence correctly?

I'm still waiting for ...

A. ... him to explain. ☐

B. ... his explanation. ☐

C. ... his explaining. ☐

7 Right or wrong?

A. I tried to **prevent him making** a big mistake. ☐

B. I tried to **prevent him from making** a big mistake. ☐

8 Which verb form(s) can complete the sentence (in British English)?

I think your car...

A. ... needs servicing. ☐

B. ... needs to be serviced. ☐

C. ... wants servicing. ☐

▶

9 Which statement about these two sentences is true?

I'm proud **of having passed** my exams.

I'm proud **to have passed** my exams.

A. They are both right and both mean the same. ☐
B. They are both right but have different meanings. ☐
C. One is right and the other one is wrong. ☐

10 Which option(s) can complete the sentences correctly?

A. I object .... (*paying, to paying, pay, to pay*) such a high price for petrol.
B. I look forward .... (*seeing, to seeing, see, to see*) her again soon.
C. As well as .... (*speaking, to speaking, speak, to speak*) Spanish, I also speak French and some Russian.

11 Which verb form(s) can complete the sentence correctly?

I remember .... my keys this morning, but I can't find them.

A. to have taken ☐
B. to take ☐
C. taking ☐

12 Is this sentence right or wrong? If it's wrong, correct it.

After she had finished her speech, the President went on giving medals to the soldiers. ⎵

....

13 Is this sentence right or wrong? If it's wrong, correct it.

We regret informing passengers that the 11.30 train is running an hour late. ⎵

....

14 Right or wrong?

A. We don't permit **parking** in front of the building. ⎵
B. We don't permit **people parking** in front of the building. ⎵
C. We don't permit **people to park** in front of the building. ⎵
D. **People are not permitted parking** in front of the building. ⎵
E. **People are not permitted to park** in front of the building. ⎵

15 *Passing, to pass* or both?

A. If you want to get the job, it'll mean .... all your exams.
B. He means .... all his exams first time round. ▶

16 I prefer working through my lunch break so that I can leave the office earlier.
Which is the best way to say the same thing?

A. I like **working** through my lunch break. ☐
B. I like **to work** through my lunch break. ☐

17 Right or wrong?

A. The police announced today that the **escaped** prisoner they were looking for has been recaptured. ___
B. The **questioned** burglar refused to say where he had hidden the stolen goods. ___
C. A **retired** general has criticised the government for its defence policy. ___

8 passives

1 Change the sentences into passive sentences with the same meaning, e.g.
She gave her sister the car. → Her sister was given the car.

A. I have told him to return the money by next Friday.

....

B. We are giving them another week to finish the job.

....

C. They had employed him for forty years before his retirement.

....

2 Write two passive sentences with the same meaning.
He has given the keys to his sister.

A. The keys ....
B. His sister ....

The company lent you a laptop last week.

C. You ....
D. A laptop ....

3 Which of the two passive structures in Question 2 would people most normally use?

A. The one used in A and D. ☐
B. The one used in B and C. ☐

▶

4 Right R or wrong W?

A. **I was given** this watch by my father. ⎵
B. This watch was **given me** by my father. ⎵
C. This watch was **given to me** by my father. ⎵

5 Choose the right preposition(s). (More than one may be correct.)

A. I was shocked .... (*at, by, of*) your behaviour.
B. I was worried .... (*about, by, at*) his reaction.
C. I was frightened .... (*about, at, by*) the spiders.

6 Which sounds more natural?

A. Mary wanting to tell everybody what to do surprised me. ☐
B. I was surprised by Mary wanting to tell everybody what to do. ☐

7 Right or wrong?

A. Everybody thought that she was clever. ⎵
B. That she was clever was thought by everybody. ⎵
C. It was thought by everybody that she was clever. ⎵

8 Right or wrong?

A. We believe **that he is** dangerous. ⎵
B. We believe **him to be** dangerous. ⎵
C. He **is believed to be** dangerous. ⎵
D. They **say that he is** dangerous. ⎵
E. They **say him to be** dangerous. ⎵
F. He **is said to be** dangerous. ⎵

9 *Tell, to tell* or both?

He was made .... them everything.

10 Is this sentence right or wrong? If it's wrong, correct it.

The escaped lion **is thought to be** dangerous. ⎵

....

11 *To be, being* or both?

There are understood .... more than 3,000 different languages in the world.

12 Right or wrong?

A. My suitcase **is packed** and I'm ready to go. ⎵
B. My suitcase **has been packed** and I'm ready to go. ⎵
C. There's been an accident – my car **is hit**. ⎵
D. There's been an accident – my car **has been hit**. ⎵

9 verbs: some special structures

1 Right R or wrong W?

A. **Give me back** my watch!
B. **Give back me** my watch!
C. **Give me** my watch **back**!

2 Right or wrong?

A. She **sat still**, hoping that the wasp would fly away.
B. She **spoke quiet**, hoping that the teacher wouldn't hear her.
C. He **fell awkwardly** and twisted his shoulder.
D. He **fell unconsciously** on the floor.
E. As the plane approached the runway, he **pulled** his seatbelt **tight**.

3 Is there anything wrong with this advertisement? If so, correct it.

SUPER SUDZ – WASHES YOUR DIRTIEST CLOTHES CLEANLY: EVERY TIME!

....

....

4 Jenny bought her husband a new tie.

In this sentence, what is ...

A. ... the subject? ....
B. ... the direct object? ....
C. ... the indirect object? ....

5 Right or wrong?

A. I **offered John** the plate of sandwiches.
B. I **pushed John** the plate of sandwiches.
C. She **read me** an extract from her latest book.
D. Can you **teach her** the guitar next year?
E. He **carried us** the cases to the taxi.

6 Right or wrong?

A. **We've been given** a lovely present by our manager.
B. **The new mobile phone was given** to the most successful salesperson.

7 Are the highlighted words in the replies right or wrong?

A. Pay him the money. ~ I can't **pay him**. I've got no money.
B. Sing her a song. ~ I can't **sing her**. I've got a terrible voice.
C. Play us the album you bought. ~ I can't **play you**. My speakers aren't working.

▶

8 Is this sentence right or wrong? If it's wrong, correct it.

After which of these children am I supposed to be looking? ☐

....

9 Rearrange these words to make a question.

looking found book for you you the have were

....?

10 nouns (1): singular and plural, countability, gender

1 Write the plural forms of these nouns. Can they end in *-s*, *-es* or both?

A. hero .... D. kilo ....
B. tornado .... E. volcano ....
C. piano .... F. echo ....

2 Write the missing singular forms of these nouns.

	Singular	Plural
A.	....	series
B.	....	crossroads
C.	....	headquarters
D.	....	species

3 Which word(s) can begin the sentence?

.... wishing to travel must have a valid ticket and passport.

A. People ☐
B. Peoples ☐
C. Persons ☐

4 Which of these sentences is/are right?

A. The news today **is** very bad. ☐
B. The aircraft **are** being refuelled. ☐
C. **This** new data **is** very worrying. ☐
D. I think the media **is** responsible for the problem. ☐
E. He picked up the dice and threw **it** again. ☐

▶

5 Both options are possible, but which word would be more natural in these sentences (in British English)?

A. The team really .... (*want, wants*) to win the cup this season.

B. The team .... (*consist, consists*) of eleven players, including the captain.

C. My family .... (*hope, hopes*) that we can go on holiday this summer.

6 Which of these sentences is/are right?

A. The choir gave **its** first performance last week and **they** are now planning a tour. ☐

B. The bank **isn't raising** interest rates this month but **they** might raise them next month. ☐

C. The theatre **is being renovated** during the summer, but **they** will open again in September. ☐

D. The committee, **who are** hoping to announce some important changes, **don't** want to comment at the moment. ☐

7 *Have* or *has*?

A number of people .... (*have, has*) tried to find the treasure, without success.

8 Which word(s) can make these uncountable nouns countable?

A. .... of luck
(*a piece, a hit, a bit, a strike, a stroke*)

B. .... of luggage
(*a piece, an item, a unit, a bag*)

C. .... of bread
(*a piece, a loaf, a ball, a slice, a roll*)

9 Which expression(s) can complete the sentences correctly?
She doesn't have .... for the job.

A. a big enough experience ☐

B. enough experience ☐

C. enough experiences ☐

I had .... when you didn't come back home last night.

D. frightening thought ☐

E. a frightening thought ☐

F. some frightening thoughts ☐

10 *It, them* or both?

Have you had measles before? ~ Yes. I had .... when I was eight.

▶

11 Complete the expressions using the words in the box below. (You won't need to use all of them.)

grain sheet bar tin slice drop scoop block

A. a .... of chocolate
B. a .... of rice
C. a .... of paper
D. a .... of ice
E. a .... of water
F. a .... of cake

12 Which of the options (A–F) in Question 6 above could be replaced by *piece*?

....

13 Choose the right noun from the ones in the box below. (You won't need to use all of them.)

flowers people doctors birds goats bees cards tyres

A. A flock of ....
B. A set of ....
C. A bunch of ....
D. A crowd of ....
E. A pack of ....
F. A herd of ....

14 Which is more normal here: *who* or *which*?

She had an old dog, Sam, ... always slept in her bed.

15 Which word(s) can complete the sentences correctly.

A. The ship has struck a rock. .... (*He's, She's, It's*) sinking fast!
B. Your car has lost one of .... (*his, her, its*) windscreen wipers.
C. Canada has decided to increase .... (*his, her, its*) trade with Europe.

16 Which of these sentences is/are right?

A. She is one of the most well-known **actors** of her generation. ☐
B. She has just been elected **chairperson** of our committee. ☐
C. She's the first person in her family to work as a **fireperson.** ☐

11 nouns (2): other points

1 Which word(s) can complete the sentences correctly?

A. I don't know the answer, but I'm going to .... (*do, make, have*) a guess.

B. I try to .... (*do, have, go for*) a run every day.

C. I'll .... (*do, have, take*) a think and then I'll let you know.

D. She .... (*makes, does, gives*) a bit of singing, but she doesn't like having a big audience.

2 Which two options sound most natural?

A. Let's **swim** before lunch. ☐
B. Let's **have a swim** before lunch. ☐
C. Do you do any sport? ~ Yes, I **swim** every day. ☐
D. Do you do any sport? ~ Yes, I **have a swim** every day. ☐

3 If both Joe and Ann are the children's parents, which sentence is right: A or B?

A. Joe**'s** and Ann**'s** children get on really well. ☐
B. Joe and Ann**'s** children get on really well. ☐

4 Which expressions(s) can finish the questions correctly?

What do you think of ...

A. ... the company management? ☐
B. ... the company's management? ☐
C. ... the management of the company? ☐

5 Which is more usual?

A. He's the husband of the woman who you met at the conference last year. ☐
B. He's the woman who you met at the conference last year's husband. ☐

6 Have you read John's novel?
What does this probably mean?

A. John wrote the novel. ☐
B. The novel belongs to John. ☐

7 The soldier's punishment was severe.
What does this probably mean?

A. The soldier punished someone severely. ☐
B. The soldier was severely punished. ☐ ▶

8 Which of these possessive forms are possible?

A. I didn't believe **the girl's story**. ☐
B. I can't remember **the street's name**. ☐
C. I'm afraid **the house's roof** is leaking. ☐
D. It looks like **the dog's leg** is broken. ☐
E. I could only get seats at **the theatre's back**. ☐
F. **The plan's importance** is clear to everyone. ☐
G. **The train's arrival** was delayed by an hour. ☐

9 Which expression(s) can end the sentence correctly?

We're expecting ...

A. ... a delay of twenty minutes. ☐
B. ... a twenty-minute delay. ☐
C. ... twenty minute's delay. ☐
D. ... twenty minutes' delay. ☐

10 Right R or wrong W?

A. a five-litre can ___
B. a five-litres can ___
C. a one-litre bottle ___
D. a litre bottle ___
E. a two-thirds share ___
F. a three-quarter length coat ___

11 Which sounds more natural: A or B?

A. We bought **three dollars' worth** of popcorn. ☐
B. We bought popcorn **worth three dollars**. ☐

12 Right or wrong?

A. yesterday's news ___
B. last Sunday's match ___
C. 1997's events ___

13 Describe this organization using just four words.

A group set up to campaign for the relief of debt.

It's a ....

14 Right or wrong?

A. Prisoners always look forward to receiving **home letters**. ___
B. I've kept all the **love letters** my girlfriend sent me. ___
C. He had a **disappointment feeling** at not getting the job. ___
E. I ate **kangaroo meat** for the first time last month. ___ ▶

Adv

15 Which option is best in each sentence?

A. He bought his wife .... (*a gold ring, a golden ring, a ring of gold*) for their wedding anniversary.

B. The inscription said: 'Fifty years of .... (*gold, golden*) memories.'

C. The flowers were like .... (*a gold carpet, a carpet of gold*).

12 pronouns

1 Normal N, very informal I or wrong W?

A. My parents they are retired now. ⌴

B. It's a beautiful city, Venice. ⌴

2 *She*, *her* or both?

A. Nobody but .... knows the secret.

B. Everybody except .... can come.

3 Which reply or replies can be used correctly?

Great news! I got that job I wanted.

A. ~ Clever you! ☐

B. ~ Intelligent you! ☐

C. ~ Lucky you! ☐

4 Right R or wrong W?

Why don't .... go to the cinema tonight?

A. you and I ⌴

B. I and you ⌴

C. we ⌴

5 Right or wrong?

I love you for ...., not for your money.

A. you ⌴

B. what you are ⌴

C. yourself ⌴

6 Right or wrong?

A. My sister and I phone **each other** every day. ⌴

B. My sister and I phone **one another** every day. ⌴

C. They often borrow **each other's** clothes. ⌴

D. They often borrow **one another's** clothes. ⌴

▶

7 How can you improve this sentence?

They divorced each other this year.

....

8 *Any one, anyone, every one* or *everyone*?

A. You can't borrow more than four books from the library at .... time.

B. I hope .... has had enough to eat.

C. .... of the apples I bought yesterday was rotten.

9 Right or wrong?

I'm looking for a new sports car. I'd like ...

A. ... **one** with a sun roof. ☐

B. ... **a one** with a sun roof. ☐

C. ... **fast one** with a sun roof. ☐

D ... **a fast one** with a sun roof. ☐

10 Which sounds more natural?

A. I don't like **these** much. ☐

B. I don't like **these ones** much. ☐

11 Which sentence ending(s) is/are possible?

A mother's job is harder than ...

A. ... a father's. ☐

B. ... a father's one. ☐

C. ... that of a father. ☐

D. ... the one of a father. ☐

12 Which sounds most natural in conversation: A, B or C?

A. Strangers **are not liked** in my village. ☐

B. **One doesn't like** strangers in my village. ☐

C. **They don't like** strangers in my village. ☐

13 Which is the best option for each sentence?

A. I can't help you, ... (*how, however*) busy you are.

B. .... (*What, Whatever*) happens, I still want to be your friend.

C. I don't understand .... (*how, however*) you can drink such strong coffee.

D. He takes a photo of his children with him .... (*where, wherever*) he goes.

14 Right or wrong?

A. **Whichever laptop** you buy, make sure it isn't too heavy. ☐

B. **Whoever people** you meet, always try to be as friendly as possible. ☐

C. **Whatever she says** to you, you must do what we agreed. ☐

▶

15 Right or wrong?

A. I'll agree to **whatever you want**. ⌴
B. **Whatever you want** is fine with me. ⌴
C. **Whoever gets the job** will have a difficult time. ⌴
D. **Whoever you give the job to** will have a difficult time. ⌴

16 What does this sentence mean?
The actor playing Hamlet is Norbert Smythe, **whoever that may be**.

A. I don't care which actor is playing Hamlet. ☐
B. I've never heard of Norbert Smythe. ☐

17 Are the replies right R, wrong W or possibly impolite I?
Would you like potatoes or rice?

A. ~ However. ⌴
B. ~ Whichever. ⌴
C. ~ Whatever. ⌴

18 Don't you have any doubts .... about his new girlfriend?
Which of these can be added?

A. at all ☐
B. whatever ☐
C. whatsoever ☐

13 determiners (1): articles, possessives and demonstratives

1 Right R or wrong W? If a sentence is wrong, correct it.

A. **The my** cousin is George Clooney. ⌴

....

B. ~ What, not **the** George Clooney? ⌴

....

C. ~ Yes, that's right. George Clooney, **actor**. ⌴

....

2 Which expression(s) can end the sentence correctly?
She's got some ...

A. ... great books in her collection. ☐
B. ... beautiful little toes. ☐
C. ... wonderful ideas. ☐

▶

3 Which expression(s) can end the sentence correctly?
The school trip to the mountains was great, but ...

A. ... **the most children** got very tired. ☐
B. ... **most of the children** got very tired. ☐
C. ... **the most of the children** got very tired. ☐

4 Which of these sentences are right?

A. **Child** needs to feel secure. ☐
B. **A child** needs to feel secure. ☐
C. **Children** need to feel secure. ☐
D. **A tiger** is in danger of becoming extinct. ☐
E. **The tiger** is in danger of becoming extinct. ☐
F. **Tigers** are in danger of becoming extinct. ☐

5 *School, the school* or both?

A. I left .... when I was sixteen.
B. I left .... by the back entrance so nobody would see me.

6 Which expression(s) are right?
Can you use chopsticks or would you prefer to eat with ...

A. ... a knife and a fork? ☐
B. ... a knife and fork? ☐
C. ... knife and fork? ☐

I didn't realise that Bill and Helen were ...

D. ... a husband and a wife ☐
E. ... a husband and wife ☐
F. ... husband and wife. ☐

7 Right or wrong?

A. Have you got **cheaper sort of radio**? ___
B. Have you got **a cheaper sort of radio**? ___
C. Have you got **a cheaper sort of a radio**? ___

8 Which of these sentences is/are right?

A. **Man and woman** were created equal. ☐
B. **Men and women** need to be able to work together. ☐
C. Previously, fire fighting wasn't seen as **a woman's** job. ☐
D. How did **Man** first discover fire? ☐

9 Right or wrong?

A. Rome is lovely **in spring.** ___
B. Rome is lovely **in the spring.** ___
C. **The spring** I spent in Rome was lovely. ___

▶

10 Right or wrong?

A. **Violin** is a difficult instrument.

B. She studied **violin and piano** at the music school.

C. The recording features Wilson **on violin** and Fernandez **on piano**.

11 Is this sentence right or wrong? If it's wrong, correct it.

She appears regularly **on radio** and **on TV**, but what she likes best is working **in theatre**.

12 Right or wrong?

A. They appointed her **the Defence Minister**.

B. Who is **the defence minister** in the new government?

13 *By, by the* or both?

A. I get paid .... hour.

B. You can order our eggs .... phone.

C. We sell our eggs .... dozen.

14 Which of these should begin with the definite article? Write in *The* if necessary.

A. .... United Kingdom

B. .... France

C. .... Chelsea Football Club

D. .... Houses of Parliament

15 Right or wrong?

A. Could I have a copy of *The Times*, please?

B. Professor Wilkins published an article in *Nature* last month.

16 These are all examples of abbreviated style. Rewrite them as full sentences, with the correct articles inserted.

A. Open packet at other end.

B. See diagram on page 26.

C. Take car to garage; pay phone bill; call dentist.

D. *MAN ATTACKED AT WATERLOO STATION WAS OFF-DUTY POLICEMAN*

▶

17 Right or wrong?

A. Bill is a friend **of Ann's**. ⎵

B. Bill is a friend **of hers**. ⎵

C. Is Ann a friend **of your father**? ⎵

D. Is Ann a friend **of your father's**? ⎵

18 Which is more natural in this sentence: *this* or *that*?

I really don't like .... new boyfriend of yours.

19 Are these sentence endings formal F, normal N or wrong W?

A dog's intelligence is much greater than ...

A. ... a cat's. ⎵

B. ... the one of a cat. ⎵

C. ... that of a cat. ⎵

14 determiners (2): other determiners

1 Which of these sentences is/are correct?

A. **All that I have** is yours. ☐

B. **All what I have** is yours. ☐

C. **All I have** is yours. ☐

D. **All** is yours. ☐

E. She lost **everything that she owned**. ☐

F. She lost **all that she owned**. ☐

G. She lost **everything**. ☐

H. She lost **all**. ☐

2 What does this sentence mean?

I wanted to please him, but **all I did** was to make him angry.

A. Everything that I did made him angry. ☐

B. Making him angry was the only thing I did. ☐

3 Which ending(s) can be used correctly?

I don't like this green door. I think we should paint it ...

A. ... another colour. ☐

B. ... a completely other colour. ☐

C. ... a completely different colour. ☐

4 What does this sentence mean?

I don't read **just any** book.

A. I don't read any books at all. ☐

B. I only read books that interest me. ☐

C. I read more than one book at a time. ☐

5 Is this sentence possible: yes Y or no N?

Each student wore what **they** liked best. ⎵

▶

6 Which expressions can complete the sentence correctly?

I've got five brothers, and .... is different.

A. each ☐
B. each one ☐
C. each of them ☐

7 Which is better: *each* or *every*?

A. .... member of the team had a short meeting with the manager.
B. .... member of the team desperately wanted to win.
C. They've lost nearly .... match they've played this season.

8 Is the reply right R or wrong W? If it's wrong, correct it.

What will your mother think? ~ That's **the least of** my worries. ⎵

....

9 What do the two sentences mean? Choose from A or B and C or D.

Arsenal hasn't got **the least chance** of winning the cup this season.

A. Arsenal hasn't got any chance at all of winning the cup this season. ☐
B. Arsenal will not be the worst team this season. ☐

I was not **in the least** upset by his bad temper.

C. I wasn't at all upset by his bad temper. ☐
D. I was extremely upset by his bad temper. ☐

10 In which of these sentences is *little* used correctly?

A. They had little hope. ☐
B. Their hope was little. ☐
C. It's little difficult. ☐
D. It's a little difficult. ☐
E. It was painted by a little-known artist. ☐
F. We have a little-liked boss at the moment. ☐

11 Right or wrong?

A. I hate this job **more and more** every year. ⎵
B. You haven't cooked enough potatoes. You need to cook **more and more**. ⎵

12 *Most, the most* or both?

They all talk a lot, but your little girl talks ....

13 That is **most** generous of you.
What does this sentence mean?

A. You have never been so generous before. ☐
B. You have been extremely generous. ☐

▶

14 When Jim's with his friends, **he mostly** talks about football.
What does this sentence mean?

A. Jim talks about football most of the time, but not always. ☐
B. Jim's the person out of all his friends who talks most about football. ☐

15 Can you improve this sentence?
He's got many men friends but he doesn't know many women.

....

16 Which of these sentences would be best to use in an essay?

A. **Many** people are worried about rising prices. ☐
B. **A lot of** people are worried about rising prices. ☐
C. **Plenty of** people are worried about rising prices. ☐

17 Which person is probably in more of a hurry: A or B?

A. Sorry, I can't stop. **I haven't got any time** to talk. ☐
B. Sorry, I can't stop. **I've got no time** to talk. ☐

18 Can you improve this sentence?
He's got no wife and no child.

....

19 Which of these are possible?

A. There **are no** completely harmless brands of cigarettes. ☐
B. There **aren't any** completely harmless brands of cigarettes. ☐
C. **Not any** brands of cigarettes are completely harmless. ☐

20 Which of these uses of *some* is/are normal N?

A. Bring **some food** in case we get hungry. ___
B. The President appealed for **some food** for the earthquake victims. ___

21 Right or wrong?

A. Mary's new boyfriend is **some** musician. I'd never heard of him or his band, but I heard him play last week and it was really bad. ___
B. That was **some** party! I'm so glad Sarah invited me; I really enjoyed myself. ___

22 One of these sentences is unusual. Which one? How would you change it?

A. I spent **a bit too much** money last month. ☐
B. You're asking **much too many** questions. ☐
C. I've had **rather too many** glasses of wine tonight. ☐

....

15 adjectives and adverbs

1 Right R or wrong W?

A. He's **only** a child. ___
B. He's a **mere** child. ___
C. That child is **only**. ___
D. That child is **mere**. ___

2 Which is the most common option for each sentence?

A. How do you feel? ~ I feel very .... (*well, healthy*), thanks.
B. She looks rather .... (*ill, sick*). Is she OK?
C. He's a very .... (*fit, well*) man: he never takes time off work.

3 Which of these word orders are right?

A. Send all the **available tickets**, please. ☐
B. Send all the **tickets available**, please. ☐
C. I gave the keys to the **upstairs woman**. ☐
D. I gave the keys to the **woman upstairs**. ☐
E. It's the only **possible solution**. ☐
F. It's the only **solution possible**. ☐

4 Right or wrong?

A. She is **a person too polite** to refuse. ___
B. She is **too polite a person** to refuse. ___
C. Those **girls are too kind** to refuse. ___
D. Those **are too kind girls** to refuse. ___

5 Are the adjectives in the right order? If not, correct them.

A. She lives in a **big modern red brick** flat. ___

....

B. I bought a **new big sports Italian red** car last week. ___

....

6 Right or wrong?

A. My **last two jobs** were really boring. I hope this one will be more interesting. ___
B. First, she told me she was getting married. The **big second shock** was that the wedding is next week. ___

7 Which of these sentences is/are right?

A. The poor **has** rights, just like the rest of us. ☐
B. The poor **have** rights, just like the rest of us. ☐
C. **The problems of the poor** are often serious. ☐
D. **The poor's problems** are often serious. ☐
E. **Poor people's problems** are often serious. ☐

▶

8 Right or wrong (in informal speech)?
Which of these shirts would you like?

A. ~ I'll have three **blue ones** and two **white ones**. ⎵

B. ~ I'll have three **blues** and two **whites**. ⎵

9 Right or wrong?

A. He drove off **angrily**. ⎵

B. He parked his car near the exit **fortunately**. ⎵

C. You speak English really **well**. ⎵

D. She read the letter **slowly**. ⎵

10 Which of these adverb positions are normal?

A. **Usually** I get up early. ☐

B. I **usually** get up early. ☐

C. I get up early **usually**. ☐

D. **Always** I get up early. ☐

E. I **always** get up early. ☐

F. I get up early **always**. ☐

11 Which of these adverb positions are normal?

A. **Today** I'm going to London. ☐

B. I'm going **today** to London. ☐

C. I'm going to London **today**. ☐

D. **Soon** everything will be different. ☐

E. Everything will **soon** be different. ☐

F. Everything will be different **soon**. ☐

12 Which of these sentences sound(s) more natural?

A. It **certainly looks** like rain. ☐

B. It **looks certainly** like rain. ☐

C. I **have never** been to the circus. ☐

D. I **never have** been to the circus. ☐

E. It **probably is** too late now. ☐

F. It **is probably** too late now. ☐

13 Which continuation(s) is/are right?
I don't trust politicians.

A. I have **never** and I will **never**. ☐

B. I **never** have and I **never** will. ☐

C. **Never** I have and **never** I will. ☐

14 Which of these sentences sound(s) more natural?

A. I **definitely** feel better today. ☐

B. **Definitely** I feel better today. ☐

C. Her train is **perhaps** late. ☐

D. **Perhaps** her train is late. ☐

▶

15 Is this sentence right or wrong? If it's wrong, correct it.

I will completely have finished by this time tomorrow. ____

....

16 Which is the right continuation: A or B?

Your mother **only** needs a drink.

A. She already has something to eat. ☐
B. Everybody else has one. ☐

17 Rearrange the sentence in Question 16 (*Your mother only needs a drink*) so that it can go before the continuation you thought was wrong.

....

16 comparison

1 Right R or wrong W?

A. She's the **politest** child I know. ____
B. Lucy is definitely the **most polite** child in the class. ____
C. Jones is the **most common** surname in Wales. ____
D. The **commonest** reason given for absence from work is flu. ____

2 Which word(s) can complete the sentence correctly?

He's .... friendly as she is.

A. as ☐
B. so ☐
C. not as ☐
D. not so ☐

3 Which sounds most natural: A, B or C?

A. You ought to rest **as much time** as possible. ☐
B. You ought to rest **for as much** as possible. ☐
C. You ought to rest **as much** as possible. ☐

4 Which word(s) can complete the sentence correctly?

It's .... as cold as yesterday.

A. almost ☐
B. not nearly ☐
C. just ☐
D. like ☐
E. nothing like ☐
F. every bit ☐
G. exactly ☐
H. not quite ☐

5 Which sounds more natural: A or B?

I used to think he was clever. Now ...

A. ... I'm not **as** sure. ☐
B. ... I'm not **so** sure. ☐

▶

6 Which phrase(s) can finish the sentence correctly?
This room is …

A. … as cold as ice. ☐
B. … cold as ice. ☐
C. … as small as a cupboard. ☐
D. … small as a cupboard. ☐

7 Which phrase(s) can complete the sentence correctly?
Kylie is .... than her sister.

A. much more famous ☐
B. much more known ☐
C. much more well known ☐
D. better known ☐
E. more better known ☐

8 Right or wrong?

A. Can you drive a bit **slower**, please? ___
B. I am pleased to report that inflation has risen **more slowly** than last month. ___

9 Is this sentence right or wrong? If it's wrong, correct it.
Strawberry and chocolate are my favourite flavours, but I think chocolate is **the nicer** of the two. ___

....

10 Right or wrong?

A. **More** it is dangerous, **more** I like it. ___
B. **The more** it is dangerous, **the more** I like it. ___

11 Right or wrong?

A. The more coffee **that** you drink, the more excitable **that** you'll be. ___
B. The more coffee **that** you drink, the more excitable you'll be. ___
C. The more coffee you drink, the more excitable you'll be. ___

12 Which sounds more natural: A or B?

A. You're more stubborn than **anybody** I know. ☐
B. You're more stubborn than **everybody** I know. ☐

13 Right or wrong?

A. Your computer is **much** better than the one I bought. ___
B. Your computer is **quite** better than the one I bought. ___
C. I'm feeling **much** better after the flu I had last week. ___
D. I'm feeling **quite** better after the flu I had last week. ___
E. This is **much** the best wine I've tasted this year. ___
F. This is **quite** the best wine I've tasted this year. ___

14 Which expression(s) can complete this sentence correctly?
Your new house is .... in the street.

A. the very nicest ☐
B. the much nicest ☐
C. much the nicest ☐
D. by far the nicest ☐

17 prepositions

1 Right R or wrong W?

A. Tell me about what you're worried. [ ]
B. What a lot of trouble I'm in! [ ]

2 Rearrange the words in the box to form a complete sentence.

who she's been I've only the with love woman ever in

....

3 Formal F, normal N or wrong W?

A. Joe's the person **who I am angry with.** [ ]
B. Joe's the person **with whom I'm angry**. [ ]
C. This is the house **about that I told you.** [ ]
D. This is the house **that I told you about.** [ ]

4 Complete the sentences using the verb *learn*.

A. I'm interested .... more about my family history.
B. I was interested .... that my grandfather originally came from Russia.

5 Choose the right option for each sentence. (X = no preposition.)

A. Nobody knows **the reason** .... (*for, from, of*) the accident.
B. I don't want **to take part** .... (X, *at, in, of*) any more conferences.
C. Can you **translate** this from English .... (*at, in, into*) Greek, please?

6 Choose the right preposition(s). (More than one might be right.)

A. I feel angry .... (*about, at, with*) the terrible things my brother said to me.
B. I feel angry .... (*about, at, with*) my brother .... (*at, for, with*) saying such terrible things.

7 *At the end* or *in the end*?

I thought the film was very sad ....
It took me a long time but .... I passed all my exams.

8 Choose the right option for each sentence. (X = no preposition.)

A. When I entered .... (X, *to, into*) **the room**, he stood up.
B. We have entered .... (X, *to, into*) **an agreement** with a Korean company.
C. He's very clever, but **he lacks** .... (X, *in, to*) experience.
D. He's very clever, but **he's lacking** .... (X, *in, to*) experience. ▶

9 Which of the highlighted prepositions can be left out in informal speech?

A. I'll see you **at** about three o'clock. ☐
B. I've been here **for** three weeks now. ☐
C. How long are you staying **for**? ☐

10 Which of these expressions can begin this sentence correctly?
... we need to buy a new car.

A. According to me, ... ☐
B. According to my opinion, ... ☐
C. In my opinion, ... ☐
D. According to my wife, ... ☐
E. According to my wife's opinion, ... ☐
F. In my wife's opinion, ... ☐

11 British English Br, American English Am or wrong W?

A. What are you doing **at** the weekend? ⌴
B. What are you doing **in** the weekend? ⌴
C. What are you doing **on** the weekend? ⌴

12 Which of these uses of *along* is/are correct?

A. Her office is just **along** the corridor, on your left. ☐
B. The children were complaining all **along** the journey home. ☐
C. I was walking **along**, minding my own business, when they approached me. ☐
D. Come **along**, children. It's time to go home. ☐

13 Right or wrong? If a preposition is wrong, change it.

A. I smoke **at** home but never **in** work. ⌴

....

B. My daughter's **at** college **at** London this year. ⌴

....

C. I hate camping holidays, especially sitting **in** a tent **in** the rain. ⌴

....

D. Open your books **on** page 32 and do exercise 5 **on** the top of the page. ⌴

....

14 Right or wrong?

A. I'll be home **by** five o'clock. ⌴
B. I'll be home **by the time** you get home. ⌴

15 Right or wrong?

A. He worked **by the day** and slept **by the night**. ⌴
B. You can hire a bicycle **by the day** or **by the week**. ⌴

▶

16 What does this sentence probably mean?
He was killed **with** a heavy stone.

A. A heavy stone fell and killed him. ☐
B. Somebody used a heavy stone to kill him. ☐

17 What does this sentence mean?
As your brother, I must warn you to be very careful.

A. I'm telling you to be careful because I'm your brother. ☐
B. I'm not your brother, but I think the same as him. ☐

18 *In front of*, *in the front of* or both?

Small children shouldn't sit .... the car. It's not safe.

18 questions, imperatives and exclamations

1 Which option(s) is it possible to use: the first, the second or both?

A. Who .... (*spoke, did speak*) just now?
B. If it wasn't Peter, who .... (*phoned, did phone*) just now?
C. I've split up with my girlfriend. ~ I'm not surprised: I never .... (*liked, did like*) her.

2 Which of these questions are possible (in informal speech)?

A. You're working late tonight? ☐
B. This is your car? ☐
C. Where you are going this afternoon? ☐
D. That's the boss? ☐

3 Which of each pair of sentences can usually mean the same as the one just above them?

You're late!
A. What time is it? ☐
B. Do you know what time it is? ☐

I can't find my coat. ~ **Here's your coat, stupid!**
C. ~ What's this, then? ☐
D. ~ Here it is! ☐

What you're doing is really silly!
E. What are you doing? ☐
F. What do you think you are doing? ☐

▶

4 Right R or wrong W?

A. George's brother came, but not George. ⌴

B. Not George came, but his brother. ⌴

C. It was not George who came, but his brother. ⌴

5 SPEAKER 1: **Would it be better** for me to leave now?

SPEAKER 2: **Wouldn't it be better** for me to leave now?

SPEAKER 3: **Why shouldn't I** leave now?

Which speaker(s) definitely want(s) to leave? ....

And which speaker most wants to leave? ....

6 Which of these questions are polite invitations?

A. **Won't you** have a drink with us? ☐

B. **Why won't you** have a drink with us? ☐

C. **Why don't you** have a drink with us? ☐

D. **Would you like to** have a drink with us? ☐

E. **Wouldn't you like to** have a drink with us? ☐

7 You aren't helping us, and I think you should.
Which of these sentences mean(s) the same?

A. Can you help us for a moment? ☐

B. Can't you help us for a moment? ☐

C. You can't help us for a moment, can you? ☐

8 Do that again and you'll be in trouble!
Which of these sentences mean(s) the same?

A. Don't do that again or you'll be in trouble. ☐

B. If you do that again, you'll be in trouble. ☐

C. When you do that again, you'll be in trouble. ☐

9 Right or wrong?

A. **Get a vaccination** as soon as you can. ⌴

B. **Get vaccinated** as soon as you can. ⌴

10 Which of these question tags is/are used correctly?
Wait here for a moment, ...

A. ... can you? ☐

B. ... could you? ☐

C. ... do you? ☐

D. ... did you? ☐

E. ... will you? ☐

F. ... would you? ☐

▶

11 Which of these replies is/are right (in informal English)?
I'm absolutely furious!

A. ~ Now **let's not get** angry. ☐
B. ~ Now **don't let's get** angry. ☐
C. ~ Now **let's don't get** angry. ☐

What do you think of their policy?

D. ~ Let me think. ☐
E. ~ Let me see. ☐
F. ~ Let me consider. ☐
G. ~ Let's see. ☐

12 Right or wrong?

A. **Let there is** no doubt in your minds about our intentions. ___
B. **Let there be** no doubt in your minds about our intentions. ___
C. **Be in** no doubt about our intentions. ___
D. **Let you be in** no doubt about our intentions. ___

13 Are these exclamations right or wrong? If they're wrong, correct them.

A. He's so nice! ___ ....
B. He's a such nice boy! ___ ....
C. They talk such a rubbish! ___ ....
D. They're so kind people! ___ ....
E. This is a so nice hotel! ___ ....

14 How you've grown!
Haven't you grown!
Do these two sentences mean the same: yes Y **or no** N**?** ___

19 conjunctions

1 Which words can you take out to make the sentences shorter? E.g.
I'll pay for you if ~~it is~~ necessary.

A. If you are in doubt, you should wait and see.
B. Prepare the meat, then cook it slowly until it is ready.
C. Once I was in bed, I read for twenty minutes, then I turned out the light.

2 Right R **or wrong** W**?**

A. We came back **because** we ran out of money **and because** Ann was ill. ___
B. **Although** she was tired, **but** she went to work. ___
C. She didn't write **when** I was ill, **or when** I got married. ___

▶

3 Which of these fixed expressions is/are correct?

A. He was on his **knees and hands**, looking for the torch he had dropped. ☐
B. My dogs are always scared of **lightning and thunder**. ☐
C. His new girlfriend is so **young and pretty**. ☐

4 *And, to* or both?

A. Try .... eat something – you'll feel better if you do.
B. I'll try .... call you tomorrow.
C. Be sure .... ask Uncle Joe about his garden.

5 Carol looks as if she is rich and Harry talks as if he was rich.
Which of these statements is/are true?

A. Carol is definitely rich. ☐
B. It's possible that Carol is rich. ☐
C. It's possible that Harry is rich. ☐
D. Harry is definitely not rich. ☐

6 Which of these expressions can complete the sentence?
You can take my car .... you bring it back this evening.

A. as long as ☐
B. so long as ☐
C. on condition that ☐
D. provided ☐

7 Which is the more normal sentence: A or B?

A. Birds can fly, as well as some mammals. ☐
B. As well as birds, some mammals can fly. ☐

8 Right or wrong?

A. Smoking is dangerous, **as well as makes** you smell bad. ____
B. **As well as breaking** his leg, he hurt his arm. ____
C. I have to feed the animals **as well as look after** the children. ____

9 What does this sentence mean?
She sings as well as she plays the piano.

A. She not only plays, but also sings. ☐
B. Her singing is as good as her playing. ☐

10 Right or wrong?

A. You can't go home before **I've signed** the letters. ____
B. He went out before **I had finished** the sentence. ____
C. She left before **I could ask** for her phone number. ____

▶

11 Which option(s) can complete the sentence correctly?
Hold it in both hands .... Mummy does.

A. as ☐
B. how ☐
C. like ☐
D. the way ☐

12 Which expression(s) can complete the sentence correctly?
It's time .... a new car.

A. for to buy ☐
B. for us to buy ☐
C. we bought ☐

13 Which sentences mean the same: A and B, B and C, or all three?

A. **Now** Phil's arrived, we can eat. ☐
B. **Once** Phil's arrived, we can eat. ☐
C. **When** Phil's arrived, we can eat. ☐

14 Right or wrong?

A. It's **far time** you got a job. ____
B. It's **high time** you got a job. ____
C. It's **long time** you got a job. ____

15 Which of these sentences is/are correct?

A. **Now** the exams are over, I can enjoy myself. ☐
B. **Now that** the exams are over, I can enjoy myself. ☐
C. **Once** I've finished my exams, I'll be able to enjoy myself. ☐
D. **Once that** I've finished my exams, I'll be able to enjoy myself. ☐

16 Which of these sentences is/are correct?

A. **Whether you like it or not**, I'm coming anyway. ☐
B. **Whether or not you like it**, I'm coming anyway. ☐
C. **Whether you like it or whether not**, I'm coming anyway. ☐
D. **Whether you like it or whether you don't**, I'm coming anyway. ☐

17 *If*, *whether* or both?

A. I'm not sure .... I'll have time.
B. .... I'll have time, I'm not sure at the moment.
C. There was a big argument about .... we should move house.
D. They can't decide .... to get married now or wait.

20 *if*

1 Right R or wrong W (in British English)?

A. If I knew her name, I **would** tell you. ⌴
B. If I knew her name, I **should** tell you. ⌴
C. If I knew her name, **I'd** tell you. ⌴

2 How could you make this question more polite by changing two words?

Will it be all right if I bring a friend?

....

3 Which sounds better: *could* or *might*?

A. If you behave yourself, I .... buy you an ice cream.
B. If I had a bigger car, I .... take all four of you to the shops.
C. If you asked me nicely, I .... do the washing-up.
D. If I knew where she lived, I .... return her phone, which she left on the table.

4 Which is/are possible?

TOUR GUIDE: Now if you .... me, we will now visit the Great Hall.

A. all follow ☐
B. will all follow ☐
C. would all follow ☐

Which sounds most polite: A, B or C? ⌴

5 Which expression(s) can complete the sentence correctly?

If you .... in the area, please come and see me.

A. should be ☐
B. would be ☐
C. happen to be ☐
D. should happen to be ☐

6 Right or wrong?

A. I'll work late tonight **if it's necessary**. ⌴
B. I'll work late tonight **if necessary**. ⌴
C. **If you are in doubt**, ask me for help. ⌴
D. **If in doubt**, ask me for help. ⌴

7 Right or wrong?

A. I'll finish this report **if** it takes me all night. ⌴
B. I'll finish this report **as if** it takes me all night. ⌴
C. I'll finish this report **even if** it takes me all night. ⌴ ▶

8 Which is closest in meaning: A or B?
If I'm angry, it's because you lied to me.

A. The only reason I'm angry is because you lied to me. ☐
B. I'm not sure whether I'm angry but, if I am, it's because you lied to me. ☐

9 Which of these expressions can replace *if* in the sentence below?
You can have Friday off **if** you work on Saturday.

A. providing that ☐
B. provided that ☐
C. on condition that ☐
D. supposing that ☐
E. as long as ☐
F. so long as ☐
G. on condition that ☐

21 indirect speech

1 A, B, or both?
Didn't you hear me? ...

A. ... I asked you how old you **are**. ☐
B. ... I asked you how old you **were**. ☐

2 Which verb form(s) can complete the sentence correctly?
He says he .... to stay very late.

A. doesn't want ☐
B. didn't want ☐
C. hasn't wanted ☐

3 Which verb form(s) can complete the sentence correctly?
DIRECT: 'What do I need?'
INDIRECT: She asked what ... .

A. ... she needs. ☐
B. ... she needed. ☐
C. ... does she need. ☐
D. ... did she need. ☐

4 Right R or wrong W?

A. He **said he would** write every day, if he could. ___
B. He **promised he would** write every day, if he could. ___
C. He **said to** write every day, if he could. ___
D. He **promised to** write every day, if he could. ___

▶

5 **Which expression(s) can complete the sentence correctly?**

DIRECT: 'What should I do next?'

INDIRECT: He asked me what … .

A. … he should do next. ☐
B. … to do next. ☐
C. … he should have done next. ☐

6 **Which expression(s) can complete the sentence correctly?**

I suggested ………… the main car park.

A. that he should try ☐
B. him to try ☐
C. that he try ☐
D. trying ☐

7 **Which expression(s) can complete the sentence correctly?**

The driver ………… the town centre.

A. asked that I wanted ☐
B. asked if I wanted ☐
C. asked whether I wanted ☐
D. said that I wanted ☐
E. said if I wanted ☐
F. said whether I wanted ☐

22 relatives

1 **Right R or wrong W?**

A. Tuesday's **the only day that is possible** for our meeting. ___
B. Tuesday's **the only day possible** for our meeting. ___

2 **Right or wrong?**

A. Where's the girl **who** sells the tickets? ___
B. Where's the girl **that** sells the tickets? ___
C. This is Naomi, **who** sells the tickets. ___
D. This is Naomi, **that** sells the tickets. ___

3 Jane's having a party for the people in the office, who are friends of hers.

Is the writer saying …

A. … that all the people in the office are Jane's friends? ☐
B. … that Jane has only invited those people in the office who are her friends? ☐

4 **Right or wrong?**

A. She was a star **whose** face was on magazine covers around the world. ___
B. It was a meeting **whose** purpose I didn't understand. ___

5 **Right or wrong?**

A. I'll give you **what help I can**. ___
B. I'll give you **any help that I can**. ___

▶

6 ***Which, That* or *What*?**

.... money he has comes from his family.

7 Which two sentences would it be better to use in a formal written report?

A. The people **who** live next door reported a disturbance. ☐
B. The people **that** live next door reported a disturbance. ☐
C. This is the room the two burglars **were caught in**. ☐
D. This is the room **in which** the two burglars **were caught**. ☐

8 Which of the sentence endings is/are possible?
I can't think of anybody ...

A. ... to invite. ☐
B. ... whom to invite. ☐
C. ... to play tennis with. ☐
D. ... whom to play tennis with. ☐
E. ... with whom to play tennis. ☐

9 Right or wrong?

A. Did you like **the wine which we drank** last night? ___
B. Did you like **the wine we drank** last night? ___
C. I poured him **a glass of wine, which he drank** at once. ___
D. I poured him **a glass of wine, he drank** at once. ___

10 Which sounds more natural: A or B?

A. Have you got something **which** belongs to me? ☐
B. Have you got something **that** belongs to me? ☐

23 special sentence structures

1 Is this sentence right or wrong? If it's wrong, correct it.

It is essential for the papers to be ready before Thursday. ___

....

2 Which sentence sounds more natural: A or B?

A. How many unhappy marriages there are is very surprising. ☐
B. It is very surprising how many unhappy marriages there are. ☐

3 Right R **or wrong** W**?**

A. It **looks if** we're going to have trouble with Ann again. ___
B. **It looks as if** we're going to have trouble with Ann again. ___
C. **It looks as though** we're going to have trouble with Ann again. ___
D. **It will be a pity if** we have to ask her to leave. ___

▶

4 Which of these sentences is/are possible (in a formal written style)?

A. She was very religious, **as were** most of her friends. ☐
B. I felt very nervous, **but were not worried** my friends. ☐
C. So ridiculous **did she look** that everybody burst out laughing. ☐

5 Which of these sentences is/are right?

A. We cannot cash cheques under any circumstances. ☐
B. Under no circumstances we can cash cheques. ☐
C. Under no circumstances can we cash cheques. ☐

6 Which of these is more likely to be used in a children's story?

A. A great castle stood in front of the children. ☐
B. In front of the children stood a great castle. ☐

7 Right or wrong (when telling a story)?

A. I stopped the car and **up walked a policeman**. ____
B. The door opened and **out came Angela's boyfriend**. ____

8 Right or wrong?

A. I have always paid my bills and I always **will pay them**. ____
B. I have always paid my bills and I always **will**. ____

9 Choose the right option(s) for each sentence. (One or both might be possible.)

A. She didn't know where she was .... (*when, when she*) woke up.
B. She wanted to stay awake .... (*but, but she*) fell asleep in the end.
C. She had no idea .... (*why, why she*) was there.

10 Which of these sentences is/are possible (in informal English)?

A. Peter started first, and then Colin started. ☐
B. Peter started first, then Colin started. ☐
C. Peter started first, then Colin. ☐

11 Make these informal spoken sentences more formal by putting back the missing words, e.g.
Wife's on holiday. → My wife's on holiday.

A. Car's running badly. ....
B. Must dash! ....
C. Seen Joe? ....
D. Keeping well, I hope? ....
E. Nobody at home. ....
F. Careful what you say! Children in the room. ....
....

▶

12 Make the sentences more emphatic by filling the gaps, using the words in the box. (You won't need to use all of them.)

indeed much so very did himself

A. I wasn't expecting to hear from the Managing Director, but I ________ get a letter from him.
B. The letter was obviously written by the Managing Director ________ .
C. He wrote to me the ________ next day after he received my letter.
D. He was much, ________ more apologetic than I expected he would be.
E. I was very surprised ________ .

13 Phil isn't the chairman; he's the secretary.
Which of these other ways of emphasising is/are possible?

A. The secretary is what Phil is. ☐
B. What Phil is is the secretary. ☐

14 *Is, are* or both?

A. What we want ________ some respect.
B. What we want ________ some of those cakes.
C. It is the students who ________ angry.

15 I thought you'd decided not to come to the party!
Which is the most normal reply?

A. ~ No. **What it was** was that the car broke down. ☐
B. ~ No. **What happened** was that the car broke down. ☐
C. ~ No. **It** was that the car broke down. ☐

24 spoken grammar

1 Which words can you leave out in informal spoken English? E.g.
~~The~~ car's running badly. **~~It~~** doesn't like cold weather.

A. There's nobody at home – my wife's on holiday.
B. You're keeping well, I hope. Have you seen Joe?
C. Did you enjoy the film? ~ I couldn't understand a word of it.
D. Be careful what you say – there are children listening.

2 Which of these sentences is/are possible in informal spoken English?
When are you coming to see us?

A. ~ **I'm coming** to see you tomorrow, I hope. ☐
B. ~ **Am coming** to see you tomorrow, I hope. ☐
C. ~ **Coming** to see you tomorrow, I hope. ☐

▶

3 Choose the right option for each sentence.

A. It's no good, ... (*is, isn't*) it?
B. It's hardly rained at all this summer, ... (*has, hasn't*) it?
C. There's little we can do about it, ... (*is, isn't*) there?

4 What does this sentence mean?
You couldn't lend me a pound, could you?

A. You weren't able to lend me a pound when I asked you. ☐
B. Could you lend me a pound, please? ☐

5 Are these replies right R or wrong W in informal spoken English? If they're wrong, correct them.

A. You didn't phone Debbie last night. ~ **No, but I did this morning.** ⎵

....

B. I think she likes cakes. ~ **Yes, she really likes.** ⎵

....

C. Is she happy? ~ **I think she is.** ⎵

....

D. Have you got a light? ~ **I think I have.** Yes, here you are. ⎵

....

E. That job didn't take him long to do. ~ **It certainly didn't.** ⎵

....

6 Complete each response with a two-word reply question, e.g.
It was a terrible party. ~ Was it? ~ Yes, it was.

A. We had a lovely holiday. ~ .... ?~ Yes, we went to China.
B. I've got a headache. ~ Oh dear, ... ? I'll get you an aspirin.
C. John likes that girl next door. ~ .... ? He's much older than her.
D. I don't understand. ~ .... ? I'm sorry, I'll explain it again.
E. It was a lovely concert. ~ Yes, ... ? I really enjoyed it, too.

7 Which expression(s) can end this sentence correctly?
Louise can dance beautifully, and ...

A. ... so her sister. ☐
B. ... so can her sister. ☐
C. ... so her sister can. ☐

▶

8 Fill in the right word to complete the sentence correctly.

A. I've lost their address. ~ So .... I.
B. I was very tired and so .... the others.
C. We live in a small village. ~ So .... my parents.
D. My daughter just wants to make money. ~ So .... my brother when he was her age, and now he's a millionaire.

25 topic-related language

1 Right R or wrong W?

A. 30 March 2004 ⌊___⌋
B. 30 March, 2004 ⌊___⌋
C. 30th March 2004 ⌊___⌋
D. March 30, 2004 *(American English)* ⌊___⌋

2 Which of these ways of writing dates in figures is/are correct?

A. 30/3/04 ☐
B. 30-3-04 ☐
C. 30,3,04 ☐
D. 30.3.04 ☐

3 Which of these ways of saying dates is/are normally correct (in British English)?

1905
A. 'nineteen hundred and five' ☐
B. 'nineteen O five' ☐
C. 'nineteen five' ☐

2005
D. 'two thousand and five' ☐
E. 'two thousand O five' ☐
F. 'two thousand five' ☐
G. 'twenty five' ☐

▶

4 Jim Walton is a professional footballer. Here are some of the different ways that people might write to him or talk to him.

Jim	sir	Dear Sir
Mr Jim	Mr Jim Walton	Walton
Jim Walton		

Match the form of address with the most appropriate title. (Use each of the titles in the box only once. You won't need all of them.)

A. Waiter in a restaurant: '*Excuse me,* .... *. I think you've dropped your wallet.'*
B. Sports commentators and members of his team: .... *had a fantastic game on Saturday.'*
C. Members of the public: '*Can you see the man in the corner? Isn't that the footballer* .... *?'*
D. Someone writing a letter who doesn't know his name. ....
E. A friend: ' .... *are you coming to the party next week?'*
F. The first line of the address in a letter sent to him. ....

One of the forms of address in the box is wrong. Which one?

....

5 Complete the table.

Country/ region	Adjective	Person	Population
Brazil	Brazilian	a Brazilian	the Brazilians
A. Norway			
B. Sweden			
C. Iraq			
D. Thailand			
E. Poland			
F. Turkey			
G. Japan			

6 Which of these ways of asking who someone is on the phone can be used correctly (in British English)?

A. **Who is that**, please? ☐
B. **Who is this**, please? ☐
C. **Who's there**, please? ☐
D. Excuse me. **Who are you?** ☐
E. Excuse me. **Who am I speaking to?** ☐
F. Excuse me. **Who is that speaking?** ☐

▶

7 Choose the right option for each sentence.

A. What's the .... (*dial code, dialling code*) for Bristol?
B. How do I get an .... (*outside, external*) line?
C. I'd like to make a .... (*charge reversed, reverse charge*) call.
D. I think you've got the .... (*false, wrong*) number.
E. I can't hear you – you're .... (*breaking up, cracking up*).

8 Are these expressions used by a switchboard operator right or wrong? Correct the ones that are wrong.

A. One moment, please. ⎣⎦
....
B. Hold the line, please. ⎣⎦
....
C. Hang on, please. ⎣⎦
....
D. I'm trying to connect you. ⎣⎦
....
E. I'm passing you through now. ⎣⎦
....
F. I'm afraid the number is occupied. ⎣⎦
....
G. I'm afraid there's no reply from his post. ⎣⎦
....

9 Which of these ways of saying times are normal in British English?

8.07

A. seven minutes past eight ☐
B. seven past eight ☐
C. eight oh seven ☐

07:10

D. ten after seven ☐
E. ten past seven ☐
F. ten past seven o'clock ☐

2.35

G. twenty-five **of** three ☐
H. twenty-five **to** three ☐
I. twenty-five **before** three ☐
J. twenty-five **till** three ☐

10 What does this question mean?
What time do you make it?

A. What time is it by your watch? ☐
B. What time are you coming? ☐

▶

11 Which way(s) of giving times is/are right?

A. The train is scheduled to leave at ....
(*five forty-five, seventeen forty-five*).

B. Meet me in the café at ....
(*half past three, fifteen thirty*).

C. The official briefing begins at ....
(*two o'clock, fourteen hundred*).

26 spelling, contractions and punctuation

1 In which sentence(s) is/are capital letters used correctly?

A. He teaches at a University. ☐
B. He teaches at a university. ☐
C. He teaches at Oxford University. ☐
D. He teaches at Oxford university. ☐
E. I think the Prime Minister is attending the summit. ☐
F. How is the French prime minister elected? ☐

2 Change these words to adverbs, e.g.

easy → easily .

A. dry ....
B. shy ....
C. sly ....
D. noble ....
E. tragic ....
F. public ....
G. comic ....

3 Right R or wrong W?

A. She's been **out-of-work** since last March. ☐
B. He's an **out-of-work** miner. ☐

4 Which spelling(s) is/are right: the first, the second or both?

A. replacable	☐	replac**e**able	☐
B. couragous	☐	courag**e**ous	☐
C. charging	☐	charg**e**ing	☐
D. judgment	☐	judg**e**ment	☐
E. acknowledgment	☐	acknowledg**e**ment	☐
F. likable	☐	lik**e**able	☐
G. milage	☐	mil**e**age	☐

▶

5 Right or wrong?

A. Normally July is much **drier** than June. ☐

B. We've just bought a new washing machine and clothes **drier**. ☐

6 Right or wrong? Correct any mistakes.

A. The horse I was **betting** on **gallopped** towards the finishing post. ☐

....

B. An **upseting** atmosphere has been **developing** among the staff since we last met. ☐

....

7 Is the spelling right or wrong? Correct any mistakes.

What happened in the kitchen just now? ~ I beleive Keith seized the sieve from Neil. ☐

....

8 Are the highlighted vowels pronounced differently in any of these words? If so, in which word(s)?

A. **O**NE ☐
B. **O**NCE ☐
C. C**OU**PLE ☐
D. C**OU**NTRY ☐
E. SH**OU**LD ☐
F. EN**OU**GH ☐
G. BL**OO**D ☐
H. D**OE**S ☐

9 And are the highlighted vowels pronounced differently in any of these words? If so, in which word(s)?

A. B**I**CYCLE ☐
B. B**I**OLOGY ☐
C. B**I**TTERNESS ☐
D. B**U**Y ☐
E. **I**DEA ☐
F. SOC**I**ETY ☐

10 Which of these contracted forms is/are written correctly (in British English)?

A. 'You**'ll** be surprised,' she said. ☐
B. 'Your mother**'ll** be surprised,' she said. ☐
C. We**'ve** decided to split up. ☐
D. John and I**'ve** decided to split up. ☐

▶

11 Which – if any – of the contracted forms in each group is/are pronounced with a different vowel sound from the others (in British English)?

A.	**we**'d □	**we**'ll □	**we**'re □	**we**'ve □
B.	**they**'d □	**they**'ll □	**they**'re □	**they**'ve □
C.	**a**ren't □	c**a**n't □	h**a**sn't □	sh**a**n't □
D.	c**oul**dn't □	**ough**tn't □	sh**oul**dn't □	w**oul**dn't □

12 Is this sentence right or wrong? If it's wrong, correct it.

I asked her if she would be so kind as to tell me what time it was? ____

....

13 What goes here ▒ ? A comma (,), a colon (:) or no punctuation (leave blank)?

A. We need three kinds of support ▒ economic, moral and political.
B. If you are ever in London ▒ come and see us.
C. Come and see us ▒ if you are ever in London.
D. We decided not to go on holiday ▒ we had too little money.
E. The cowboy was tall ▒ dark and handsome.
F. This is an expensive ▒ ill-planned ▒ wasteful project.
G. HAMLET ▒ To be, or not to be...

14 Is the highlighted punctuation right or wrong?

A. It is a fine idea**;** let us hope that it is going to work. ____
B. The blue dress was warmer**,** on the other hand**,** the purple one was prettier. ____
C. You may use the sports facilities subject to the following conditions**;** that your subscription is paid regularly**;** that you arrange for all necessary cleaning to be carried out**;** that you undertake to make good any damage. ____

15 Right or wrong?

A. She had very little to live on, but she would never have dreamed of taking what was not hers. ____
B. She was poor but she was honest. ____

16 Which is/are possible here ▒ ? A colon (:), a dash (–) and/or a comma (,)?

There are three things I can never remember ▒ names, faces, and I can't remember the third thing. ....

17 Which of the quotation marks is/are written correctly?

A. **'**My least favourite sentence,**'** said Fiona, **'**is **"**It's time to go home**"**.**'** □
B. **'**My least favourite sentence,**'** said Fiona, **'**is **'**It's time to go home**'**.**'** □
C. **"**My least favourite sentence,**"** said Fiona, **"**is **'**It's time to go home **'**.**"** □

▶

Adv

18 Are these ways of using an apostrophe normally right R, unusual U, or wrong W?

A. It is a nice idea, but there are a lot of if's. ___
B. He writes b's insead of d's. ___
C. It was in the early 1960's. ___
D. My sister and I both have PhD's . ___
E. *JEAN'S – HALF PRICE!* ___

27 words (1): similar words

1 *Alternate, alternative, alternately* or *alternatively*?

A. You could go by air or .... you could drive there.
B. Meetings in our Brussels office take place .... in Flemish and French.
C. I'm busy on Tuesday: can we find an .... date?
D. She's working from home on .... days: Mondays, Wednesdays and Fridays.

2 *Altogether* or *all together*?

A. With the tip, the bill comes to a hundred dollars ....
B. I'm afraid the decorating isn't .... finished.
C. Let's sing her *Happy Birthday To You.* .... now!

3 *Born, borne* or *bore*?

A. He was .... in Germany in 1925 to Swiss parents.
B. I .... his insults patiently.
C. She .... four children in six years.
D. The king's body was .... away to the cathedral.
E. Hundreds of children are .... deaf each year.

4 Which is another way of saying *I don't care at all*: A, B or C?

A. I couldn't care. ☐
B. I couldn't care at all. ☐
C. I couldn't care less. ☐

5 I don't care for modern paintings.
Which means the same as this sentence: A, B or C?

A. I'm not interested in modern paintings. ☐
B. I'm not responsible for looking after modern paintings. ☐
C. I don't like modern paintings. ☐ ▶

6 Which of these can mean the same as *Take care!* ?

A. Be careful! ☐
B. Don't forget! ☐
C. Listen to me! ☐
D. Goodbye! ☐

7 *Continual, continuous, continually* or *continuously*?

A. The shop has been open .... since seven this morning.
B. Must you .... interrupt me?
C. Shoplifting is a .... problem for us.

8 *Economic* or *economical*?

A I've changed to a small car. It's much more .... than my old one.
B. The country is facing a number of serious .... problems.
C. Why did you buy that cheap aftershave? ~ I was trying to be ....

9 *Effective* or *efficient*?

A The post isn't very .... in my neighbourhood; my letters are often two days late.
B My new car is very .... My petrol bills have almost halved.
C That cleaner you gave me was very .... It got rid of all those wine stains.

10 *Lay, lie, laid* or *lied*? (More than one might be possible.)

A. Carefully, I .... the papers on the table and left the room.
B. Do something useful – don't .... in bed all day!
C. .... down your gun and put your hands in the air!
D. I .... down and closed my eyes. Soon I was asleep.

11 *Loud, loudly* or *aloud*?

A. He was talking so .... that I had a headache.
B. When she reads .... , her pronunciation is excellent.
C. 'How .... do you want us to play?' asked the band.

12 *Shade, shadow* or both?

I'm really hot! Let's find some .... to sit in. ▶

13 ***Some time, some times, sometime,* or *sometimes*? (More than one might be possible.)**

A. I'm afraid it'll take .... to repair your car.
B. Let's have dinner .... next week.
C. .... you can be very irritating.
D. Let's meet next week. I'll email you .... when I know I'll be free.

14 ***Whose* or *who's*?**

A. Do you know anyone .... going to France in the next few days?
B. .... is the blue sports car in the managing director's parking space?
C It's a decision .... consequences are still not clear.

28 words (2): other confusable words

1 ***Agreed, accepted* or both?**

I .... to meet them here.

2 ***Almost, nearly* or *practically*? (More than one might be possible.)**

A. I've .... finished
B. I've very .... finished.
C. He's got a strange accent; he sounds .... foreign to me.
D. She's .... never at home.
E. He eats .... nothing.

3 ***Back* or *again*?**

A. I don't think she got your letter: you'd better write ....
B. If I write to you every week, will you write .... ?
C. The bicycle you sold me is too small. Can I sell it .... to you?

4 **Which of these sentences is/are correct?**

A. I stood up, and then **I sat back down.** ☐
B. I stood up, and then **I sat down again.** ☐
C. I'll be **back in the office** on Monday. ☐
D. I'll be **in the office again** on Monday. ☐

▶

5 *Big, large* or *great*? (More than one might be possible.)

A. We lived in a .... house: there were six bedrooms.
B. Most people agree that Mahatma Gandhi was a .... man.
C. What's your new flat like? ~ There's not much space, but it's really .... I love living there.
D. If you think that, you're making a very .... mistake.
E. I have .... respect for her ideas.

6 *Brought up, educated* or both?

These children are very badly .... They're always shouting and fighting each other.

7 Right R or wrong W?

A. What shall we eat tonight? ~ Well, I could **make** an omelette. ☐
B. What shall we eat tonight?' ~ 'Well, I could **do** an omelette. ☐
C. He's old enough to **make** his own bed now. ☐
D. I'll **do** the vacuuming once I've **done** the beds. ☐

8 Which is the best option: *finally, at last, in the end* or *at the end*?

A. Steve has .... found a job.
B. Steve has found a job ....
C. .... ! Where the hell have you been?
D. First, release the handbrake. Then, check your mirror. .... start the car.
E. Every question should have a question mark ....
F. We looked at lots of different makes of car but, ... it was a question of price.

9 Right or wrong (in British English)?

A. We **let** our house to some students. ☐
B. We **rented** our house to some students. ☐
C. We **hired** our house to some students. ☐
D. They **let** a house from us. ☐
E. They **rented** a house from us. ☐
F. They **hired** a house from us. ☐

10 *Ill, sick* or both (in British English)?

A. I'm looking after my .... mother.
B. I didn't come to work yesterday because I was ....
C. I think it's food poisoning: I was .... three times in the night.

11 Fill in the missing day in the reply.

Fred is coming **in** two days' time and then Sue is arriving three days **later**.

~ OK. Today is Monday. That means Sue's arriving on .... ▶

12 ***Last week, the last week* or both?**

A. I was ill .... but I'm OK this week.

B. I've had a cold for .... and I feel terrible.

C. In .... of our holidays something funny happened.

13 It's only June now, but I'm already looking forward to January 1st. **Which sentence follows this one: A or B?**

A. **Next year** will be wonderful. ☐

B. **The next year** will be wonderful. ☐

14 **Is *maybe* or *perhaps* better here?**

[Political speech]: 'This country is facing what is .... the greatest crisis in its history.'

15 **Right or wrong?**

A. Cars can park on both sides of the **road**. ___

B. Cars can park on both sides of the **street**. ___

C. The **road** out of our village goes up a steep hill. ___

D. The **street** out of our village goes up a steep hill. ___

16 **Right or wrong?**

A. My watch is five minutes **slow**. ___

B. My watch is five minutes **early**. ___

C. My watch is five minutes **fast**. ___

D. My watch is five minutes **late**. ___

17 **Which sounds better: *talk* or *speak*?**

A. He's giving a .... on local history.

B. His throat was very sore so he was unable to ....

C. May I .... to Mr Walker, please?

D. Why do you .... such nonsense?

E. Now I am delighted to introduce Professor Martha Wilson, who has kindly agreed to .... on recent developments in genetics.

F. And now here's our old friend Jim Brown, who's going to .... to us about his mountaineering expedition to the Himalayas.

18 **Which sounds better here: *thankful* or *grateful*?**

I'm so .... that we avoided the accident on the motorway.

29 words (3): other vocabulary problems

1 *After, afterwards* or both?

I'm going to do my exams, and .... I'm going to study medicine.

2 Is this sentence right or wrong? If it's wrong, correct it.

After the theatre we had supper and went to a nightclub; then **after all** we went home. ☐

....

3 Right R or wrong W?

A. He's **alike** his brother. ☐
B. He's got two very **alike** daughters. ☐
C. His two daughters are very much **alike**. ☐

4 Right or wrong?

A. Don't ask me money. ☐
B. Don't ask me my name. ☐
C. They're asking £500 a month for the flat. ☐

5 I asked John to go home.
What does this mean?

A. I wanted John to go home. ☐
B. I asked John if I could go home. ☐
C. It can mean either A or B. ☐

6 What does the reply mean?

Did you enjoy the play? ~ I'm afraid I didn't like it **at all**.

A. I didn't like all of it. ☐
B. I didn't like any of it. ☐

7 Which option(s) is/are correct: the first, the second or both?

A. I suppose the job was very boring. ~ .... (*On the contrary, On the other hand*), it was very exciting.
B. 'Short' is the .... (*contrary, opposite*) of 'long'.

8 Which question(s) can this answer: A, B or both?

~ No, it's my first time here.

A. Have you ever been to Scotland? ☐
B. Have you ever been to Scotland before? ☐

▶

9 *Always, ever* or both?

A. I shall .... remember you.
B. I've loved you .... since I met you.

10 Right or wrong?

A. How soon **will you be** finished? ☐
B. How soon **will you have** finished? ☐
C. I went to get the car from the garage, but they **weren't** finished. ☐
D. I went to get the car from the garage, but they **hadn't** finished. ☐

11 Which of these sentences is/are normally correct?

A. He **gave a cough** to attract my attention. ☐
B. He **gave me a smile** to show he was pleased. ☐
C. Do you think my idea will work? ~ Let's **give it a try**. ☐
D. Sorry if I upset you. ~ I didn't **give it a thought**. ☐

**12 Which of the words (A–H) can be used in this expression?
Let's go for a ...**

A. ... drink. ☐
B. ... drive. ☐
C. ... walk. ☐
D. ... run. ☐
E. ... ski. ☐
F. ... sing. ☐
G. ... swim. ☐
H. ... play. ☐

13 Which of the highlighted verbs could be replaced by *know* without changing the meaning of the sentence?

A. How did you **find out** that she was married? ☐
B. I **understand** exactly what you mean. ☐
C. I want to travel round the world and **get to know** people from different countries. ☐
D. He's from Liverpool, as you can **tell** from his accent. ☐

14 Is the reply right or wrong? If it's wrong, correct it.

You were very noisy when you came in last night. ~ **I know it**, I'm sorry.

☐ ....

15 Which of these sentences is/are correct?

A. I'll **let you know** my holiday dates next week. ☐
B. Could you **let me have** the bill for the car repair? ☐
C. Don't **let go of** Mummy's hand! ☐
D. After questioning, **he was let go** home. ☐
E. After questioning, **he was let to go** home. ☐

▶

16 Which of these sentences is/are correct?

A. **It's very likely that I'll be** late tonight. ☐
B. **I'm very likely to be** late tonight. ☐
C. **I'm very likely being** late tonight. ☐
D. **I think I'll very likely be** late tonight. ☐

17 Right or wrong?

A. People seem to be very depressed **nowadays.** ___
B. I don't like the **nowadays** fashions. ___

18 Which of the highlighted expressions could be replaced by *once*?

A. Come up and see me **sometime.** ☐
B. We must go walking **one day.** ☐
C. I met the Queen **on one occasion**, when she visited my company. ☐

19 Right or wrong?

A. I noticed that the **opposite man** was looking at me. ___
B. His brother was fighting on the **opposite side.** ___

20 Right or wrong?

A. **Part** of the roof was missing. ___
B. **A large part** of the roof was missing. ___

21 Which of the highlighted expressions could be replaced by *presently*?

A. The Manager is **currently** on holiday. ☐
B. She will be back in the office **soon.** ☐

22 Use FOUR of the words from the box to complete the sentences.

leftovers remainder remains rest rests

A. There were .... of the meal all over the floor.
B. I'm afraid that supper tonight is .... from lunch.
C. There are four chocolates for Penny, four for Joe and the .... are mine.
D. If you divide 100 by 12, the .... is 4.

Is the one you didn't use a correct or incorrect word?

....

23 *Already, still* or *yet*?

A. Have you .... finished? That was quick!
B. Don't eat the pears – they're not ripe ....
C. I want to go out. Is it .... raining?

▶

24 STUDENT A: I've studied French for many years, but I can't speak it **yet**.
STUDENT B: I've studied French for many years, but I **still** can't speak it.

Which student is more confident: A or B? ____

25 ***Still, yet*** **or both?**

We have .... to hear from the bank about our loan.

26 PASSENGER A: The train has been cancelled. What **should** we do now?
PASSENGER B: The train has been cancelled. What **are we supposed to** do now?

Which passenger is probably angrier: A or B? ____

27 People are talking about the famous footballer, Derek Beckenham. Is their use of *supposed* right or wrong?

A. He's **supposed to be** completely fit throughout the season. Otherwise, he won't play at his best. ____
B. He's **supposed to be** extremely rich. People say he won't need to work at all once he retires. ____

28 Which of these sentences is/are correct?

A. We'll have to wait **for the photos to be** ready. ☐
B. We'll have to wait **that the photos are** ready. ☐
C. I **waited** a very long time for her to answer. ☐
D. I **waited for** a very long time for her to answer. ☐
E. Please **await** me here. I won't be a minute. ☐
F. We're still **awaiting** instructions from army headquarters. ☐

29 ***To prove, of proving*** **or both?**

There's no way .... that he was stealing.

30 Right or wrong?

A. We are fighting to defend our **way of life**. ____
B. The train is my favourite **way of transport**. ____

LEVEL 3

Expert

LEVEL 3 Expert

1 present and future verbs

1 Right R or wrong W?

A. Why **is he hitting** that dog? ___
B. **I'm going** to America about once a month. ___
C. **We're going** to a lot of concerts these days. ___

2 Right or wrong?

A. My job's **getting** less and less interesting. ___
B. Most jobs **get** less and less interesting as time goes by. ___
C. The universe **is expanding**, and has been since its beginning. ___

3 Right or wrong?

A. She doesn't like to be disturbed when **she's working**. ___
B. When the post comes **I'm usually having** breakfast. ___
C. You look lovely when **you smile**. ___
D. You look lovely when **you're smiling**. ___

4 What is the difference between these two sentences?

A. **I look forward** to hearing from you.
B. **I'm looking forward** to hearing from you.

---

5 Three of these sentences mean more or less the same. Which one is different?

A. **Are you doing** the shopping tomorrow? ☐
B. **Are you going to do** the shopping tomorrow? ☐
C. **Will you do** the shopping tomorrow? ☐
D. **Will you be doing** the shopping tomorrow? ☐

6 Is/Are any of these sentences possible? If so, which?

A. **I'm wanting** a taxi to the station now. ☐
B. I told the receptionist that **I was wanting** a taxi to the station. ☐
C. **I'll be wanting** a taxi to the station at 6.00 tomorrow morning. ☐

7 Which of these is/are right: A, B or both?

A. **I hear** you're getting married. ☐
B. **I've heard** you're getting married. ☐

8 Which of these sentences are right?

A. Our house **is getting** new windows this winter. ☐
B. Our house **is going to get** new windows this winter. ☐
C. Their new house **is looking** over the river. ☐
D. Their new house **is going to look** over the river. ☐

▶

9 In order to hire a car, you have to fill in a form which contains the following sentence:
The hirer **shall be** responsible for maintenance of the vehicle.
Is this use of *shall*

A. normal? ☐
B. typical of very formal language? ☐
C. more common in American English than in British English? ☐
D. a mistake? ☐

10 What do you think of the future structure in this sentence?
I'm going to be working late tomorrow.

A. It's normal? ☐
B. It's correct but unusual? ☐
C. It's incorrect? ☐

11 Choose the best explanation of Ann's reply.

JOE: Do you think John will come to the meeting?
ANN: No, he'll have forgotten.

A. He's already forgotten. ☐
B. He may remember now, but he'll forget before the meeting takes place. ☐

2 past and perfect verbs

1 Which of these is/are right?

A. I **played** a lot of tennis when I lived in Bath. ☐
B. I **was playing** a lot of tennis when I got to know Peter, so I was pretty fit. ☐
C. I **was having** lunch with the President the other day, and he said ... ☐
D. John **was saying** that he still can't find a job. ☐

2 Which is the best continuation: A, B or C?
I'm busy today, so ...

A. ... I'd rather you will come tomorrow. ☐
B. ... I'd rather you come tomorrow. ☐
C. ... I'd rather you came tomorrow. ☐

3 Are these continuations right R or wrong W?
It's time you ...

A. ... go home. ___
B. ... went home. ___
C. ... should go home. ___

▶

4 Are these continuations right or wrong?
I wish I ...

A. ... **know** how to fix my computer. ☐
B. ... **knew** how to fix my computer. ☐
C. ... **would know** how to fix my computer. ☐

5 Here are three invitations. In what way are they different?

A. I **wonder** if you'd like to have dinner with me.
B. I **wondered** if you'd like to have dinner with me.
C. I **was wondering** if you'd like to have dinner with me.

---

6 'I got that job last year because I was a good driver.'
Is the speaker still a good driver?

A. Probably. ☐
B. Probably not. ☐
C. No. ☐

7 Are these continuations right or wrong?
In an ideal society you would always be free to say ...

A. ... what you would think. ☐
B. ... what you would be thinking. ☐
C. ... what you thought. ☐

8 Which of these continuations are right: A, B or both?
You look as if you ...

A. ... have seen a ghost. ☐
B. ... had seen a ghost. ☐

9 Are the tenses right or wrong in the following sentences?

A. Look what John's **given** me! ☐
B. Who **gave** you that? ☐

10 Which is more natural?

A. **Barbara's phoned** today. She wants to borrow your bike. ☐
B. **Barbara phoned** today. She wants to borrow your bike. ☐

11 What do you think of this way of using of the present perfect?
Police **have arrested** 45 suspected terrorists in countrywide raids **last weekend**.

A. It's normal. ☐
B. It's unusual. ☐
C. It's completely incorrect. ☐

▶

12 Some of the following adverbs are used with a simple past tense more often in American English than in British English. Which?

afterwards already before ever just really then today yesterday yet

13 Which of these sentences is/are wrong?

A. **You're looking** much better since your operation. ☐
B. **You've been looking** much better since your operation. ☐
C. We visit my parents every week since **we bought** the car. ☐
D. We visit my parents every week since **we've bought** the car. ☐
E. We visit my parents every week since **we've had** the car. ☐

14 Not all of these rules are true. Which are the good ones?

A. Use the present perfect for recent actions, and the simple past for actions that took place longer ago. ☐
B. Use the present perfect for finished actions that have some present importance, and the simple past for other finished actions. ☐
C. Use the present perfect for unfinished actions and the simple past for finished actions. ☐
D. Use the simple past, not the present perfect, when you talk about a definite time. ☐
E. Use the simple past, not the present perfect, when you talk about a finished time. ☐

15 You're older than I thought!

Why not ... *than I have thought*?

16 Why is a present perfect progressive used in A and not in B?

A. The universe **has been expanding** steadily since its origin.
B. The castle **has looked** down on the city of Newlyn for the last 900 years.

17 Choose the correct verb form.

I .... some clothes to be cleaned. Are they ready?

A. left ☐
B. was leaving ☐
C. had left ☐

18 Why is a past perfect used in A and not in B?

A. When I **had written** my letters I did some gardening.
B. When I **opened** the door the children ran in.

3 auxiliary verbs

1 Right R or wrong W?

A. You**'re being** stupid.
B. I **was being** depressed, so I went to see Maureen.
C. This job **is being** difficult.
D. Angela's **being** difficult again.

2 Right or wrong?

A. **Do be** careful.
B. **Don't be** shy.
C. Children – if you **don't be** quiet, you'll go straight to bed.

3 Are these ways of completing the sentence right or wrong?

I thought we were saying goodbye forever, but we .... again years later.

A. met
B. were to meet
C. would meet

4 Which use(s) of *do so* is/are natural?

A. I need to speak to John. I'll try to **do so** tomorrow. ☐
B. Ann's been to Patagonia, and I'd love to **do so**. ☐
C. I think you're wrong, and I've always **done so**. ☐

5 Which expression(s) can complete the sentence correctly?

Sue looks happy. ~ Yes, she .... a new boyfriend.

A. must have ☐
B. must have got ☐

6 One of these is wrong. Which?

A. **Do you ever have** time to go to London? ☐
B. **Have you ever got** time to go to London? ☐
C. **Do you have** time to go to London this weekend? ☐
D. **Have you got** time to go to London this weekend? ☐

7 Choose the correct form.

A. I had a very strange thing .... to me when I was 14. (*happen, happened, happening*)
B. We had a gipsy .... to the door yesterday. (*come, came, coming*)
C. I looked up and saw that I had water .... through the ceiling. (*drip, dripped, dripping*)

▶

8 What does this sentence mean?
I had my application form checked by the secretary.

A. I got the secretary to check my application form. ☐
B. The secretary took my application form and checked it. ☐
C. Both of the above meanings are possible. ☐

9 Right or wrong?

A. **I'm having** to work very hard at the moment. ___
B. What time **have you got** to be back home? ___

10 One of these structures is formal F, one is normal N and one is wrong W. Which is which?

A. At no time did she contact the police. ___
B. At no time she contacted the police. ___
C. She did not contact the police at any time. ___

4 modal verbs (1): *can, could, may, might, must / have to, should*

1 Which verb(s) can complete the sentence?
He says that we .... use the car park.

A. can ☐
B. may ☐
C. might ☐

2 Which replies are right?
Where's Sarah?

A. ~ She **can** be with Joe. ☐
B. ~ She **may** be with Joe. ☐
C. ~ She **could** be with Joe. ☐
D. ~ She **might** be with Joe. ☐

3 Which modal verb(s) can complete the sentence?
We .... go camping this summer; I'm not sure.

A. may ☐
B. might ☐
C. can ☐
D. could ☐

4 Are these uses of *may* right R or wrong W?

A. **May you be** in London next week? ___
B. **Do you think you may be** in London next week? ___
C. **I may be** in London next week. ___

▶

5 Are these uses of *can* right or wrong?

A. She **can win** the race next month if she really tries. ____
B. I **can speak** French well in another three months. ____

6 Are these uses of *could* right or wrong?

A. I **could find** a really nice dress in the sale yesterday. ____
B. I **could play** the piano quite well when I was younger. ____
C. When I went into the kitchen **I could** smell something burning. ____

7 What do you think about these two sentences?

She **speaks** Greek very well.
She **can speak** Greek very well.

A. They mean the same. ☐
B. They have different meanings. ☐
C. One of them is incorrect. ☐

8 What does John's reply mean?

ANN: I don't know what to give Alex for his birthday.
JOHN: You **can always** give him a book token.

A. You can give him a book token every year. ☐
B. You give him a book token every year. ☐
C. You can give him a book token if you can't think of anything better. ☐

9 Right or wrong?

A. We **could have spent yesterday** on the beach if we'd planned things better. ____
B. We **could have spent today** on the beach if we'd planned things better. ____

10 Right or wrong?

A. **May I** park here? ____
B. **May everybody** park here? ____
C. **Can I** park here? ____
D. **Can everybody** park here? ____

11 Right or wrong?

You were stupid to try climbing up the cliff. You **may have killed** yourself. ____

12 Right or wrong?

A. A female crocodile **may** lay 30–40 eggs. ____
B. A female crocodile **can** lay 30–40 eggs. ____
C. In those days a man **might** be hanged for stealing a sheep. ____
D. In those days a man **could** be hanged for stealing a sheep. ____ ▶

13 What does this sentence mean?

He **may be** clever, but he hasn't got much common sense.

A. I agree that he's clever, but ... ☐
B. Perhaps he's clever, but ... ☐
C. He's clever sometimes, but ... ☐

14 Right or wrong?

A. Ann wasn't at the station. She **may have missed** her train. ____
B. John isn't answering his phone. He **may have gone** out by now. ____
C. By the end of this year I **may have saved** enough money to go to America. ____

15 One of these sentences is less natural than the others. Which?

A. I **must** do some more work. I want to pass my exam. ☐
B. I **have to** do some more work. I want to pass my exam. ☐
C. In my job I **must** work from 9 to 5. ☐
D. In my job I **have to** work from 9 to 5. ☐

16 Right or wrong?

A. When you leave school **you'll have to** find a job. ____
B. **I've got to** go for a job interview tomorrow. ____

17 What do you think about these two sentences?

Ellie isn't in her office. She **had to go** home early.
Ellie isn't in her office. She **must have gone** home early.

A. They have different meanings. (If so, what?) ☐

....

....

B. They mean the same. ☐
C. One of them is incorrect. ☐

18 One of these sentences is wrong. Which one?

A. He only left the office five minutes ago. He **can't be** home yet. ☐
B. He only left the office five minutes ago. He **mustn't be** home yet. ☐
C. She walked past without saying hello. She **can't have seen** us. ☐
D. She walked past without saying hello. She **mustn't have seen** us. ☐

19 Which verb form(s) can complete the sentence correctly?

It's important that he .... to the police.

A. should talk ☐
B. talks ☐
C. talk ☐

▶

20 Which verb form(s) can complete the sentence correctly?
It's surprising that she .... so much make-up.

A. should put on ☐
B. puts on ☐
C. put on ☐

21 Which is/are the best explanation(s) of the sentence?
Jake should get the manager's job, I think.

A. I think Jake will definitely get the job. ☐
B. I think Jake will very probably get the job. ☐
C. I think Jake deserves to get the job. ☐

5 modal verbs (2): other modals and semi-modals

1 What is the best explanation of this use of *will*?
She **will sit** talking to herself for hours.

A. It refers to habitual behaviour. ☐
B. It predicts future behaviour. ☐
C. It describes a wish. ☐

2 What do you think about this stressed use of *will*?
She **WILL** fall in love with the wrong people.

A. It refers critically to habitual behaviour. ☐
B. It refers neutrally to habitual behaviour. ☐
C. It makes a critical prediction of future behaviour. ☐

3 What is the best paraphrase of this sentence?
You **WOULD** tell Mary about the party – I didn't want to invite her.

A. You wanted to tell Mary about the party ... ☐
B. You were going to tell Mary about the party but you didn't ... ☐
C. It was typical of you to tell Mary about the party ... ☐

4 *Would, used to* or both?

A. When we were kids we .... go swimming every weekend.
B. I .... have an old Volkswagen that kept breaking down.
C. Robert .... play a lot of football when he was at school.

▶

5 Right R or wrong W?

A. What **did people use** to do in the evenings before TV? ___
B. I **didn't used** to like opera. ___
C. **Used you** to play football? ___
D. You used not to like him, **used you**? ___

6 Which of these sentences is/are right?

A. **Do we need to reserve** seats on the train? ☐
B. **Need we reserve** seats on the train? ☐
C. I wonder if **I need fill in** a form. ☐
D. I know **I need fill in** a form. ☐
E. Ann **needsn't work** tomorrow. ☐

7 Right or wrong?

She **daren't tell** her husband what she thinks. ___

8 What does this mean?
I dare say Alice is going to cause trouble.

A. Alice is quite probably going to cause trouble. ☐
B. I'm not afraid to say that Alice is going to cause trouble. ☐
C. I don't know whether Alice is going to cause trouble. ☐
D. Alice is certainly going to cause trouble. ☐

6 structures with infinitives

1 Right R or wrong W?

A. He began **to slowly get up** off the floor. ___
B. He began **slowly to get up** off the floor. ___

2 Right or wrong?

A. All I did was **to give** him a little push. ___
B. All I did was **give** him a little push. ___

3 Right or wrong?

A. He's **difficult to please**. ___
B. Her pronunciation is **impossible to understand**. ___
C. My brother is **hard to learn** languages. ___
D. Iron is **easy to rust**. ___
E. This material is **impossible to catch fire**. ___

▶

4 Which of these sentences is/are right?

A. These apples are **ripe enough to pick.** ☐
B. These apples are **ripe enough to pick them.** ☐
C. This box is **too heavy to lift.** ☐
D. This box is **too heavy to lift it.** ☐

5 Which of these sentences is/are right?

A. Pat is **nice to talk.** ☐
B. Pat is **nice to talk to.** ☐
C. Pat is **nice to talk to her.** ☐
D. Her family are **easy to get on.** ☐
E. Her family are **easy to get on with.** ☐
F. Her family are **easy to get on with them.** ☐

6 Are these continuations right or wrong?
I don't think this hotel is ...

A. ... a good place to stay. ____
B. ... a good to stay place. ____

7 Right or wrong?

A. Mary needs a friend **to play with.** ____
B. Mary needs a friend **with whom to play.** ____
C. I'm looking for a field to **keep my horse in it.** ____
D. Have you got a good thriller **which to read**? ____

8 Which of these continuations is/are possible?
I'm not sure ...

A. ... who to invite. ☐
B. ... how to mend this. ☐
C. ... where to put the bottles. ☐
D. ... why to tell John. ☐
E. ... when to arrive. ☐

9 Right or wrong?

A. Are there any letters **to post**? ____
B. Are there any letters **to be posted**? ____
C. The carpets **to clean** are in the garage. ____
D. The carpets **to be cleaned** are in the garage. ____
E. John's got a lot of people **to contact.** ____
F. John's got a lot of people **to be contacted.** ____
G. Those clothes are **to wash.** ____
H. Those clothes are **to be washed.** ____

▶

10 Right or wrong?

A. The children were nowhere **to see**. ☐
B. You are **to congratulate** on your exam results. ☐
C. Nobody was **to blame** for the accident. ☐

11 Which of these continuations is/are possible?

The car was a complete wreck. ...

A. ... There was **nothing to do**. ☐
B. ... There was **nothing to be done**. ☐

12 Right or wrong?

A. I **would like to have seen** his face when he found the frogs. ☐
B. I **would have liked to have seen** his face when he found the frogs. ☐

13 Which of these sentences is/are possible?

A. Can you arrange **for the gold to be delivered** on Friday? ☐
B. I need **for you to help** me. ☐
C. She asked **for the designs to be sent** to her office. ☐
D. We'd like **for you to stay** as long as you want. ☐
E. She hates **for people to feel** sad. ☐

14 What do you feel about these two sentences?

It's important **for there to be** a fire escape at the back of the building.

It's important **that there should be** a fire escape at the back of the building.

A. There's no important difference. ☐
B. The first is wrong. ☐
C. The second is wrong. ☐

15 Which extra word makes the speaker sound more disappointed?

I came home .... **to find that** my parents had already left.

A. even ☐
B. just ☐
C. only ☐

7 *-ing* forms and past participles

1 Right R or wrong W?

A. Do you object **to working** on Sundays? ___
B. I agreed **to organising** the meeting. ___
C. I prefer cycling **to walking**. ___
D. I must get round **to doing** the filing. ___

2 Which replies are possible: A, B or both?

My girlfriend won't speak to me.

A. ~ **Try to send** her flowers. ☐
B. ~ **Try sending** her flowers. ☐

3 Right or wrong?

A. I don't intend **working** for the rest of my life. ___
B. I don't intend **to work** for the rest of my life. ___
C. She continued **screaming** until they all went away. ___
D. She continued **to scream** until they all went away. ___
E. We are committed **to help** the local children. ___
F. We are committed **to helping** the local children. ___

4 Which is the most natural continuation?

I don't like to drive fast because ...

A. ... I'm afraid **to crash**. ☐
B. ... I'm afraid **of crashing**. ☐

5 Right or wrong?

A. Before the game she felt very sure **to win**. ___
B. Before the game she felt very sure **of winning**. ___
C. The repairs are certain **to cost** more than you think. ___
D. The repairs are certain **of costing** more than you think. ___

6 Which verb forms can complete the sentences? Both may be possible.

A. I was interested .... in the paper that they had found gold in Oxfordshire. (*to read, in reading*)
B. I'm interested .... in America this summer. (*to work, in working*)

7 Which verb forms can complete the sentences? Both may be possible.

A. I glanced out of the window and saw Peter .... towards the house. (*come, coming*)
B. I once heard Menuhin .... all of Bach's unaccompanied violin sonatas. (*play, playing*) ▶

8 Which of the following expressions are NOT normal?

A. a fallen leaf ☐
B. an escaped prisoner ☐
C. an arrived train ☐
D. a developed country ☐
E. a slept child ☐
F. a vanished civilisation ☐
G. a retired policeman ☐
H. a started race ☐
I. a collapsed building ☐

9 Right or wrong?

A. He's a **well-read** man. ___
B. She's a **much-travelled** woman. ___
C. The **recently-arrived** train is the 14.50 from Hereford. ___

10 Which of these is/are possible?

A. Why **are** those cars **stopped** at the crossroads? ☐
B. **Is** John completely **recovered**? ☐
C. Where **are** you **camped**? ☐
D. I'**ll be finished** in a few minutes. ☐
E. Those days **are gone** now. ☐

11 What can Canadians who speak English be called?

A. **English-speaking** Canadians. ☐
B. **English-speaker** Canadians. ☐
C. **speaking-English** Canadians. ☐
D. **speaker-English** Canadians. ☐

12 Right or wrong?

A. We didn't reach agreement on any of the **discussed problems**. ___
B. The **questioned people** were released without charge. ___
C. **Those selected** will begin training on Monday. ___

13 Some past participles have different meanings when used before or after nouns – compare *an adopted child* and *the solution adopted*. Which two of these past participles change their meaning in the same way?

concerned estimated expected involved revised

....

14 How can the following sentences most naturally be completed: with *very*, *much* or *very much*? (More than one may be possible.)

A. She's .... admired by her colleagues.
B. The children were .... frightened by the thunder.
C. Alexander has been .... weakened by his illness.
D. We were .... surprised by Joe's response.
E. The next station is ours, unless I'm .... mistaken.

▶

15 Right or wrong?

A. Who's **the girl dancing** on the table? ☐
B. Most of **those invited** failed to turn up. ☐
C. Do you know **anyone having lost** a cat? ☐

16 Right or wrong?

A. **Looking out of the window**, the mountains seemed very close. ☐
B. **Having so little time**, there was not much I could do. ☐
C. **Generally speaking**, men can run faster than women. ☐

17 Right or wrong?

A. **Nobody having** any more to say, the meeting was closed. ☐
B. **Hands held high**, the dancers circle to the left. ☐

18 Right or wrong?

A. **If asked**, say nothing. ☐
B. **Keep refrigerated** when opened. ☐
C. She was upset **because shouted at**. ☐
D. **Once deprived** of oxygen, they die within minutes. ☐
E. Keep stirring **until cooked**. ☐

8 passives

1 Only two of the following changes from active to passive are possible. Which?

A. John resembles Peter. → Peter is resembled by John. ☐
B. A high wall encloses the garden. → The garden is enclosed by a high wall. ☐
C. Our advisers recommend further investment. → Further investment is recommended by our advisers. ☐
D. That suit doesn't fit you. → You aren't fitted by that suit. ☐
E. The government lacks confidence. → Confidence is lacked by the government. ☐

2 Complete these sentences with suitable prepositions. DON'T use *by*.

A. I was shocked .... her behaviour.
B. Ann's very frightened .... spiders.
C. We're worried .... the future.
D. I'm excited .... the possibility of getting a new job.
E. Everybody's annoyed .... you.
F. I'm surprised .... your attitude.
G. The man is known .... the police.
H. The room was filled .... thick smoke.
I. The mountains are covered .... snow.

▶

3 Right R or wrong W?

A. **I worry** when you come home late. ☐
B. **I'm worried** when you come home late. ☐
C. He fell into the river and **drowned**. ☐
D. He fell into the river and **was drowned**. ☐
E. Stop chatting – there's work **to do**. ☐
F. Stop chatting – there's work **to be done**. ☐

4 Which reply is best? Why?

How are your brothers?

A. ~ Fine. Peter's restoring an old house. ☐
B. ~ Fine. An old house is being restored by Peter. ☐

....

5 Why does this text keep changing from active to passive and back?

He **waited** for two hours; then he **was seen** by a doctor; then he **was sent** back to the waiting room. He **sat** there for another two hours – by this time he **was getting** angry. Then he **was taken** upstairs ...

....

6 Which sentence is more natural? Why?

A. John trying to tell everybody what he thought annoyed me. ☐
B. I was annoyed by John trying to tell everybody what he thought. ☐

....

7 Right or wrong?

A. The plan has been carefully looked at. ☐
B. He was thrown stones at. ☐
C. That table mustn't be put cups on. ☐
D. Your brother can't be relied on. ☐

8 Right or wrong?

A. **It was decided** to put off the meeting until the following week. ☐
B. **It is hoped** to open a new school next year. ☐
C. **It was agreed** to advertise for a new secretary. ☐
D. **It is not expected** to have difficulty in finding somebody suitably qualified. ☐

9 Right or wrong?

A. I **was asked to send** full details to the manager. ☐
B. Andrew **was chosen to be** our spokesperson. ☐
C. Doris **was wanted to be** the union representative. ☐
D. They **were told not to speak** to the press. ☐
E. Our staff **are liked to make** suggestions to the management. ☐

▶

10 Right or wrong?

A. Goethe **was considered** a genius by his contemporaries. ___
B. Alice **was elected** President of the Association. ___
C. Dr Hastings **was regarded as** an expert in criminal law. ___
D. Louis **was seen as** a sort of clown. ___
E. Janet **was called** stupid by the other children. ___
F. The house **has been made** much more attractive by the new owners. ___

11 Some ideas can be expressed with both active and passive structures with little difference. For which of the following is this true?

A. I **worry** about Chris. / I**'m worried** about Chris. ☐
B. Suddenly the door **opened**. / Suddenly the door **was opened**. ☐
C. We **concern** about Joe. / We**'re concerned** about Joe. ☐
D. My shoes **are wearing** out. / My shoes **are being worn** out. ☐
E. He fell overboard and **drowned**. / He fell overboard and **was drowned**. ☐

9 verbs: some special structures

1 Right R or wrong W?

A. Lend them to her. ___
B. Lend them her. ___
C. Lend her them. ___
D. Give it me. ___
E. She sent them it. ___

2 After some verbs (e.g. *give, send*) we can put an indirect object before a direct object:

They gave **Mrs Andrews** a medal.
I sent **Mary** some flowers.

With which of the following verbs is this structure possible?

bring carry describe donate explain push throw suggest

....

3 Phrasal verb PH or prepositional verb PR?

A. I **looked up** the street to see if Andy was coming. ___
B. I'll **think over** your suggestion. ___
C. She **turned up** the next card: it was the King of Diamonds. ___
D. Can you **look after** the kids for a few minutes? ___
E. Nobody understood why she **broke off** their engagement. ___
F. We **drove round** the town looking for a hotel. ___
G. She **changes round** all her furniture every few months. ___

▶

4 Formal F, informal I, unusual U or wrong W?

A. Joe is the person I am most angry with. ___
B. Joe is the person whom I am most angry with. ___
C. Joe is the person who I am most angry with. ___
D. Joe is the person with whom I am most angry. ___

5 Right or wrong?

A. I painted white the wall. ___
B. I painted white all the kitchen walls as well as the doors and the ceiling. ___

6 What is the difference between these two sentences?
I thought **him to be** an excellent choice.
I thought **that he was** an excellent choice.

A. Only one is correct. (Which?)
B. One is more formal. (Which?)
C. There is a difference of meaning. (What?)

---

7 Which is the most natural continuation?
Everybody found her ...

A. ... very pleasant. ☐
B. ... to be very pleasant. ☐

8 Right or wrong?

A. She made **that she disagreed clear**. ___
B. She made **clear that she disagreed**. ___
C. She made **it clear that she disagreed**. ___

9 Which is most natural?

A. She ran into the room. ☐
B. She came into the room running. ☐
C. She entered the room running. ☐

10 Right or wrong?

A. The book **reads well**. ___
B. My handmade jewellery **is selling well**. ___
C. Be careful – the table **scratches** easily. ___
D. These knives **don't polish** well. ___
E. This light bulb **won't unscrew**. ___

11 Formal F, normal N or wrong W?

A. It is essential that every child **have** the same educational opportunities. ___
B. The judge recommended that he **remain** in prison for life. ___
C. We prefer that he **do not leave** school until 18. ___ ▶

12 Formal, normal or wrong?

A. It's important that Mary **be** told at once. ⎣___⎦
B. It's important that Mary **should be** told at once. ⎣___⎦
C. It's important that Mary **is** told at once. ⎣___⎦

13 Formal, normal or wrong?

A. I wish I **was** somewhere else. ⎣___⎦
B. I wish I **were** somewhere else. ⎣___⎦

10 nouns

1 Right R or wrong W?

A. **Politics is** the art of the possible. ⎣___⎦
B. What **are** your **politics**? ⎣___⎦
C. **Mathematics is** a basic school subject. ⎣___⎦
D. **Mathematics make** me nervous. ⎣___⎦
E. **Statistics is** useful in language testing. ⎣___⎦
F. The unemployment **statistics are** disturbing. ⎣___⎦

2 Choose the correct plural form.

A. bacteriums / bacteria / bacterias ....
B. crisis / crisises / crises ....
C. criteriums / criterions / criteria / criterias ....
D. phenomenon / phenomenons / phenomena / phenomenas
....
E. stimulus / stimuluses / stimula / stimuli ....

3 Are these plurals right or wrong?

A. She spelt *necessary* with two **c's**. ⎣___⎦
B. Do you remember the **1960's**, Granddad? ⎣___⎦
C. He takes **taxi's** everywhere he goes. ⎣___⎦
D. **PC's** are getting cheaper. ⎣___⎦
E. I need a new pair of **jean's**. ⎣___⎦

4 Which plural form(s) is/are right: the first, the second or both?

A. passer-bys / passers-by ....
B. mother-in-laws / mothers-in-law ....
C. runner-ups / runners-up ....
D. court martials / courts martial ....

5 Right or wrong?

A. Can you give me back **that twenty euros** I lent you? ⎣___⎦
B. Three friends of mine **is coming** to see me this evening. ⎣___⎦
C. Thirty kilometres **is** a long way to walk. ⎣___⎦ ▶

6 Which is/are right: A, B or both?

A. Two and two **is** four. ☐
B. Two and two **are** four. ☐

7 Which forms are normal?

A. More than one person **is** going to have to find a new job. ☐
B. More than one person **are** going to have to find a new job. ☐
C. One of my friends **is** getting married. ☐
D. One of my friends **are** getting married. ☐

8 Which is/are right: A, B or both?

A. Your toast and marmalade **is** on the table. ☐
B. Your toast and marmalade **are** on the table. ☐

9 Formal F, normal N or wrong W?

A. Somebody left **their** umbrella in the office. Would they please collect it? ___
B. I had a friend in Paris, and **they** had to go to hospital for a month. ___

10 Which is/are possible: A, B or both?

A. She's one of the few women who **has** climbed Everest. ☐
B. She's one of the few women who **have** climbed Everest. ☐

11 Right or wrong?

A. The biggest time-waster in our office **is** meetings. ___
B. The biggest time-waster in our office **are** meetings. ___
C. What we need **is** a few bright young engineers. ___
D. What we need **are** a few bright young engineers. ___
E. A good knowledge of three languages **is** necessary for this job. ___
F. A good knowledge of three languages **are** necessary for this job. ___

12 Which form is natural: A, B or both?

A. Six people lost **their life** in the crash. ☐
B. Six people lost **their lives** in the crash. ☐

13 Right or wrong?

A. All documents must be accompanied by **a translation** of the **original**. ___
B. All documents must be accompanied by **translations** of the **originals**. ___
C. We usually go and see my mother **on Saturday**. ___
D. We usually go and see my mother **on Saturdays**. ___
E. **Children** may resemble both their **father** and their **mother** in different ways. ___ ▶

14 Which of these expressions are right?

A. the **accounts** department ☐
B. an **antiques** dealer ☐
C. a **shoes** shop ☐
D. a **sports** car ☐
E. a **tickets** office ☐
F. **woman**-haters ☐
G. **women** drivers ☐

15 Right or wrong?

A. Who **is** working tomorrow? ~ Phil and Pete are. ____
B. What **lives** in those little holes? ~ Rabbits do. ____

16 Right or wrong?

A. **Here's** your keys. ____
B. **There's** some children at the door. ____
C. **What's** those women talking about? ____
D. **Where's** those books I lent you? ____

17 Is there a difference between these two sentences?
None of the cures really **work**.
None of the cures really **works**.

A. No important difference. ☐
B. The first is wrong. ☐
C. The second is wrong. ☐
D. The first is more informal. ☐
E. The second is more informal. ☐

18 Right or wrong?

A. I want to stay for **another three weeks**. ____
B. We'll need **an extra ten pounds**. ____
C. She spent **a happy ten minutes** looking through the photos. ____
D. I've had **a very busy three days**. ____

19 Right or wrong?

A. I've got **too much nose** and **not enough chin**. ____
B. I haven't got **much idea** of her plans. ____
C. Have we got **enough chair** for everybody? ____
D. Do you think we have **much chance** of catching the train? ____

20 Which two of these nouns can be used in the plural?

furniture information knowledge spaghetti travel weather

....

21 Which three of these nouns can be used with the article *a/an*?

education English experience health knowledge weather

.... ▶

Expert

22 Which alternatives are right: the first, the second or both?

A. the Queen's arrival / the arrival of the Queen

B. the room's back / the back of the room

C. the page's top / the top of the page

D. John's letter / the letter of John

E. the earth's gravity / the gravity of the earth

23 Right or wrong?

A. mountain's plants
B. a book of history
C. tiredness signs

24 Right or wrong?

A. a five-litres can
B. a table's leg
C. baby clothes
D. a birdcage
E. a bird's egg
F. chicken's soup
G. sheep's wool

11 pronouns

1 Normal N, informal I or wrong W?

A. **John and me** are going skiing this weekend.
B. **Me and the kids** spent Sunday at the swimming pool.
C. **Between you and I**, I think his marriage is in trouble.

2 Right R or wrong W?

A. **I woman** know things **you man** will never understand.
B. **We women** know things **you men** will never understand.
C. **They men** will never understand things **we women** know.
D. **Us women** understand these things better than you men.

3 Formal F, normal N, informal I or wrong W?

A. **It's me that needs** your help.
B. **It is I who need** your help.

4 Normal, informal or wrong?

A. It's for **he** to decide, not me.
B. It's a good idea for **you and I** to meet soon.
C. Everything comes to **he** who waits.

▶

5 Formal, normal or wrong?

He who hesitates is sometimes lost. ____

6 All of these sentences are wrong. Why?

One speaks English in this shop.
One is knocking at the door.
In the 16th century **one** believed in witches.

....

....

7 This sentence is also wrong. Why?

One speaks a strange dialect where I come from.

....

8 Right or wrong?

A. She often talks to **herself** when she's alone. ____
B. She always takes her dog with **herself** when she goes out. ____

9 Is the use of *yourself* (instead of *you*) in these sentences necessary N, optional O or wrong W?

A. It shouldn't be difficult for a clever person like **yourself**. ____
B. I have something here that will be very interesting for **yourself**. ____
C. Why don't you give **yourself** a break from what you're doing? ____

10 Are the reflexive pronouns in these sentences necessary, optional or wrong?

A. Hurry **yourself**! ____
B. I don't always shave **myself** as soon as I get up. ____
C. She's old enough to dress **herself** now. ____
D. His book's selling **itself** well. ____
E. I feel **myself** very depressed these days. ____
F. The door slowly opened **itself**. ____
G. Concentrate **yourself**! ____

11 Which is more normal: A or B?

A. They each listened carefully to what **the other** said. ☐
B. They listened carefully to what **each other** said. ☐

12 Right or wrong?

.................................., you have to do what we say.

A. Whatever your opinions ... ____
B. Whatever your opinions are ... ____
C. Whatever are your opinions ... ____

▶

Expert

13 **Are these sentences right or wrong? If they're wrong, correct them.**

A. A good student, **however clever**, won't succeed without working hard. ⌴

....

B. An insect bite, **whatever its type**, should be treated immediately. ⌴

....

12 determiners (1): articles, possessives and demonstratives

1 **Which sentences are more natural?**

A. **Farmers** often vote Conservative. ☐
B. **The farmers** often vote Conservative. ☐
C. What has this government ever done for **farmers**? ☐
D. What has this government ever done for **the farmers**? ☐

2 **Right** R **or wrong** W**?**

A. He's studying **the** French painters. ⌴
B. He's particularly interested in **the** Impressionists. ⌴

3 **Right or wrong?**

A. She's just written a book on **African butterflies.** ⌴
B. She's just written a book on **the butterflies of Africa**. ⌴

4 **Right or wrong?**

A. I like **the** seaside. ⌴
B. I like **the** nature. ⌴
C. I go to **the** mountains every summer. ⌴
D. I like exploring **the** small towns. ⌴

5 **Right or wrong?**

A. We saw **a** wheel of a car lying by the road. ⌴
B. She kicked him on **a** knee. ⌴
C. He usually sits at **a** side of the church. ⌴
D. I'm sorry, you've got **the** wrong number. ⌴

6 **British English** Br**, American English** Am **or both** B**?**

A. Ann's **in the hospital** again. ⌴
B. What did you study **at the university**? ⌴
C. I like to read **in bed** before I go to sleep. ⌴
D. She's arriving **by train**. ⌴

▶

7 With or without *the*?

A. I was surprised at the amount of .... collected. (*money, the money*)

B. The number of .... is rising steadily. (*unemployed, the unemployed*)

8 Right or wrong?

A. I had **a toothache** last week. ☐

B. This week I've got **a cold**. ☐

C. And I expect next week I'll have **the flu**. ☐

9 Which is more natural?

A. She slapped him in **the** face. ☐

B. She slapped him in **his** face. ☐

10 Right or wrong?

A. She studied at **the** Oxford University. ☐

B. He's doing a course at **the** Exeter School of English. ☐

C. I'll be arriving at **the** Birmingham Airport. ☐

D. They were married in **the** Salisbury Cathedral. ☐

11 Are these mountain names right or wrong?

A. **the** Everest ☐

B. **the** Kilimanjaro ☐

C. **the** Matterhorn ☐

D. **the** Mont Blanc ☐

12 Is this sentence right or wrong? (If it's wrong, correct it.)

I've had **my breakfast** and the dog's had **its**. ☐

....

13 Right or wrong?

A. I didn't realise it was going to be **this** hot. ☐

B. If your boyfriend's **that** clever, why isn't he rich? ☐

C. It was **that** cold that I couldn't feel my fingers. ☐

D. The film wasn't all **that** good. ☐

E. There was **this** travelling salesman who was looking for a place to stay ... ☐

14 Which of these continuations is/are possible?

So she decided to paint her house pink. ...

A. ... **It** upset the neighbours a bit. ☐

B. ... **That** upset the neighbours a bit. ☐

C. ... **This** upset the neighbours a bit. ☐

▶

15 Which continuation(s) is/are natural: A, B or both?

I dropped the computer onto the table. ...

A. ... **It** was badly damaged – the screen was smashed. ☐
B. ... **This** was badly damaged – the screen was smashed. ☐

16 Right or wrong?

A. Tell me what you think about **that**: I thought I'd get a job in Spain for a few months. ___
B. I thought I'd get a job in Spain for a few months: tell me what you think about **that**. ___

13 determiners (2): other determiners

1 Right R or wrong W?

A. She's invited **us all.** ___
B. Who has she invited? ~ **Us all.** ___
C. Who broke the window? ~ It was **them both.** ___
D. She kissed **them each** on the forehead. ___
E. She kissed **them each.** ___
F. I bought them **two ice-creams each.** ___
G. The ice-creams cost **£1.50 each.** ___

2 Right or wrong?

A. **All the story** was completely unbelievable. ___
B. **All my family** were there for my birthday. ___
C. They stayed with us **all that week.** ___

3 Normal N, unusual U or wrong W?

All is lost! ___

4 A and B mean the same; C and D mean the same. Which are the most natural ways of expressing these ideas?

A. Every kind of bird can't fly. ☐
B. Not every kind of bird can fly. ☐
C. All Americans don't like hamburgers. ☐
D. Not all Americans like hamburgers. ☐

5 Right or wrong?

A. It rained **the whole summer.** ___
B. It rained **the whole of the summer.** ___
C. By September, **whole London** was under water. ___
D. By September, **the whole of London** was under water. ___ ▶

6 Right or wrong?

A. She doesn't care what either of her parents **says.** ___
B. She doesn't care what either of her parents **say**. ___
C. Neither of my sisters **is** married. ___
D. Neither of my sisters **are** married. ___
E. None of my friends **is** interested. ___
F. None of my friends **are** interested. ___

7 Right or wrong?

A. The plums are ripe enough **to eat**. ___
B. The plums are ripe enough **to eat them.** ___
C. The plums are ripe enough for the children **to eat**. ___
D. The plums are ripe enough for the children **to eat them**. ___

8 Two of these are right. Which?

A. She spends **half her time** in Germany. ☐
B. She spends **half of her time** in Germany. ☐
C. She spends **a half of her time** in Germany. ☐
D. She spends **the half of her time** in Germany. ☐

9 Which is/are right: A, B or both?

A. Half of my friends **live** abroad. ☐
B. Half of my friends **lives** abroad. ☐

10 Not all of these are right. Which ones are?

A. half of a mile ☐
B. half a kilo ☐
C. a half kilo ☐
D. one and a half hour ☐

11 One of these is unusual. Which?

A. a great deal of money ☐
B. a large amount of money ☐
C. a large amount of people ☐

12 Choose the correct verb form.

A. A large number of problems .... caused by poverty. (*is, are*)
B. The majority of criminals .... non-violent. (*is, are*)

13 Formal F, normal N, informal I or wrong W?

They lived **plenty of miles** from the town. ___

▶

14 Look at these sentences.

Most nurses are still women.	*Right*
~~**Most of nurses** are still women.~~	*Wrong*
Most of the/our/these nurses are still women.	*Right*
Most of them are still women.	*Right*

Which of these other determiners follow this pattern?

A. many ☐
B. a lot ☐
C. more ☐
D. some ☐

15 Which is/are right: A, B or both?

A. Who earns **most** money in your family? ☐
B. Who earns **the most** money in your family? ☐

16 *Less*, *fewer* or both?

A. I've got .... problems now than I had ten years ago.
B. I've got .... money now than I had ten years ago.

17 Right or wrong?

A. I **very much like** your hair. ____
B. We **very much appreciate** your help. ____
C. There's **very much water** coming through the ceiling. ____

18 Right or wrong?

A. A whale is **no fish**. ____
B. George is **no fool**. ____
C That's **no problem** at all. ____

19 Right or wrong?

A. It **wasn't so much** his appearance I liked **as** his personality. ____
B. She **didn't so much as** say thank you. ____

20 Why is *some* used in this sentence?
Our products are exported to **some** sixteen countries.

A. It means 'about.' ☐
B. It suggests that sixteen is not a large number in this context. ☐
C. It suggests that sixteen is an impressive number in this context. ☐
D. It means that not all of the sixteen countries import the products. ☐

14 adjectives and adverbs

1 Two of the following expressions are not correct. Which?

Secretary General   President Elect   God Almighty
Chairman Deputy   Poet Laureate   court martial
Professor Senior   Attorney General

....

2 Two of these adjectives can be used before or after nouns, but with different meanings. Which?

present   proper   different   certain   precise

....

3 Put together the two groups of words in each case (without adding any) to make one correct expression.

A. a life   different from this one

....

B. a problem   difficult to solve

....

C. some people   skilled in design

....

4 Can either or both of these expressions be written without commas?

A. a lovely, long, cool, refreshing drink ☐
B. a tall, dark, handsome cowboy ☐

5 In the following expressions, is *and* necessary N, possible P or wrong W?

A. a **cruel and vicious** tyrant ___
B. a **yellow and black** sports car ___
C. a **nice and old** woman ___
D. a **social and political** problem ___

6 Right R or wrong W?

A. The body of **the deceased** was found in the river. ___
B. **The arrested** was held at the police station overnight. ___
C. **The accused** was charged with the crime today. ___
D. The verdicts on Evans and Riley were announced: **the former** was found guilty, **the latter** not guilty. ___ ▶

7 In which two sentences is the word *aged* pronounced in the same way?

A. He has a **aged** ten. ☐

B. An **aged** man once told me an amazing story. ☐

C. He has **aged** so much since he took that job. ☐

8 Normal N, unusual U or wrong W?

A. I **probably will not** be there. ___

B. I **will probably not** be there. ___

C. I **probably won't** be there. ___

D. I **won't probably** be there. ___

E. He **probably does not** know. ___

F. He **does probably not** know. ___

G. I **do not often** have headaches. ___

H. I **often do not** have headaches. ___

9 (British English): is the word order normal N or used for emphasis E?

A. She **has certainly made** him angry. ___

B. She **certainly has made** him angry. ___

C. He **has probably arrived** by now. ___

D. He **probably has arrived** by now. ___

10 Would any of the sentences in Question 7 have different answers for American English? If so, which?

....

11 Which of these is/are natural: A, B or both?

A. They **sometimes must be** bored. ☐

B. They **must sometimes be** bored. ☐

12 *Dead* can sometimes mean 'extremely' or 'completely' (e.g. *dead drunk, dead wrong*). Can you think of any other examples?

....

13 *Clean* can sometimes mean 'completely' (e.g. *The robbers got clean away.*) Can you think of any other examples?

....

14 Right or wrong?

A. She didn't **play fair**. ___

B. They didn't **fight fair**. ___

C. He didn't **judge fair**. ___

▶

15 Right or wrong?

A. The baby's **doing fine.** ☐
B. The baby's **doing finely.** ☐

16 Which of these are adverb particles but not prepositions?

along away back down in off on out

....

17 Which of these are prepositions but not adverb particles?

at behind during from into over round under

....

15 comparison

1 What does this mean?

There are **as many as 40 students** in some of the classes.

A. Some of the classes have up to 40 students. ☐
B. Some of the classes have 40 students, and that's a lot. ☐
C. Some of the classes have exactly 40 students. ☐

2 Right R or wrong W?

A. It's as easy to do it now **as to leave** it till tomorrow. ☐
B. It's as easy to do it now **as leave** it till tomorrow. ☐

3 Right or wrong?

A. We'll get there **as soon as you do.** ☐
B. We'll get there **as soon as you will.** ☐

4 Which one of these comparative expressions is wrong?

A. The road's getting **more and more steep.** ☐
B. I'm tall, but my brother is **more tall.** ☐
C. **He's more lazy** than stupid. ☐
D. You couldn't be **more wrong.** ☐

5 Which of these are right?

A. You'll have **much more** opportunities in America. ☐
B. You'll have **many more** opportunities in America. ☐
C. You'll have **far more** opportunities in America. ☐
D. There are **far less** opportunities in this country. ☐
E. There are **many less** opportunities in this country. ☐
F. There are **many fewer** opportunities in this country. ☐
G. There are **a lot fewer** opportunities in this country. ☐
H. There are **much fewer** opportunities in this country. ☐ ▶

6 Right or wrong?

We've set up a special class for the **cleverer** students. ____

7 Which of these is/are right?

A. He explained it all carefully, but I was **none the wiser**. ☐
B. He explained it all carefully, but I was **not the wiser**. ☐
C. He explained it all carefully, but I was **none wiser**. ☐
D. He explained it all carefully, but I was **no wiser**. ☐

8 Right or wrong?

A. My grandmother can run **twice as** fast as you. ____
B. My grandmother can run **twice faster than you**. ____
C. I can run **three times as fast as you**. ____
D. I can run **three times faster than you**. ____

9 Right or wrong?

A. I spent more money **than was sensible** yesterday. ____
B. I spent more money **than it was sensible** yesterday. ____
C. There were more people at the meeting **than we had expected**. ____
D. There were more people at the meeting **than we had expected them**. ____

10 Right or wrong?

A. She was the first woman **to climb** Everest solo. ____
B. She was the first woman **who climbed** Everest solo. ____
C. Is this the first time **for you to stay** here? ____
D. Is this the first time **you've stayed** here? ____

11 Right or wrong?

A. Of all my friends, he's **nicest**. ____
B. Of all my friends, he's **the nicest**. ____
C. He's **nicest** when he's with children. ____
D. He's **the nicest** when he's with children. ____
E. Which of you can run **fastest**? ____
F. Which of you can run **the fastest**? ____

16 prepositions

Expert

1 *Above, over* or both?

A. We've got a little house .... the lake.
B. It's three degrees .... zero today.

2 One of these is common in American English Am; the other is mainly used in British English Br. Which is which?

A. Can I look **around**? ⎣⎦
B. Can I look **round**? ⎣⎦

3 *Between* or *among*?

A. I sat .... the manager and his secretary.
B. Our house is .... the woods, the river and the village.
C. She looked down and saw a strange-looking box .... the wheels of the car.
D. Her passport was hidden .... all the papers on her desk.

4 Put in the correct preposition or ✕ (= no preposition).

A. I'm not very clever .... mending things.
B. She crashed .... a tree, but she wasn't badly hurt.
C. I don't want to depend .... my parents.
D. Let's discuss .... your plans.
E. The book is divided .... three sections.
F. She's seriously lacking .... tact.
G. The photo was conclusive proof .... his innocence.
H. Geoffrey shouted .... us to come in for dinner.
I. Who's the man .... the black hat?
J. When she talks .... that voice I know I'm in trouble.

5 Normal N, informal I or wrong W?

A. Come round for a drink **Monday evening**. ⎣⎦
B. Let's **go some place** quiet. ⎣⎦
C. They're looking for **a place to live**. ⎣⎦

6 Right R or wrong W?

A. She likes **to be looked at**. ⎣⎦
B. This is a pleasant place **to live in**. ⎣⎦
C. I was astonished at the patience **she spoke with**. ⎣⎦
D. Which period did it **happen during**? ⎣⎦

▶

Expert

7 Right or wrong?

A. **For whom** is it? ___
B. **To where** shall I send it? ___
C. **About money was never spoken** in our family. ___

8 Can you correct this sentence?

The judge paid a lot of attention **to that the child was unhappy** at home.

....

9 Right or wrong?

A. Tell me **where** you went. ___
B. Tell me **about where** you went. ___
C. It depends **how** much traffic there is. ___
D. It depends **on how** much traffic there is. ___
E. I'm worried **where** she is. ___
F. I'm worried **about where** she is. ___

17 questions, negatives and imperatives

1 In these exchanges, which of the replies is/are correct?

A. I'm getting married. ~ **You're getting married?** ☐
B. She's invited 13 people to dinner. ~ **She's invited how many?** ☐
C. I've broken the fettle gauge. ~ **The what have you broken?** ☐
D. Where are you going? ~ **Where I'm going? Home.** ☐
E. Are you tired? ~ **Am I tired?** I'm exhausted. ☐

2 Right R or wrong W?

A. Who you invite is your business. ___
B. Where we stay doesn't matter. ___
C. You can eat it how you like. ___
D. I'm surprised at how fast she can run. ___

3 Right or wrong?

A. Who do think wrote this? ___
B. Who do you think that wrote this? ___
C. Who do you wish you'd married? ___
D. Who do you wish that you'd married? ___

▶

4 A and B mean the same; C and D mean the same; E and F mean the same. Which are the most natural ways of expressing these ideas?

A. I hope Alice isn't coming. ☐
B. I don't hope Alice is coming. ☐
C. I think you haven't met my wife. ☐
D. I don't think you've met my wife. ☐
E. I believe Henry's not at home. ☐
F. I don't believe Henry's at home. ☐

5 Is/are any of these sentences unnatural in conversation?

A. I believe not. ☐
B. I don't believe so. ☐
C. I suppose not. ☐
D. I don't suppose so. ☐
E. I think not. ☐
F. I don't think so. ☐
G. I hope not. ☐
H. I don't hope so. ☐

6 Formal F, normal N or wrong? W?

A. The dog seems not to like you. ___
B. She wants not to speak to anybody. ___
C. I expect not to see her for some time. ___

7 Which of the statements is/are true?

Don't tell them nothing.

A. The sentence is incorrect. ☐
B. In standard English, the sentence means 'Tell them something.' ☐
C. In all varieties of English, the sentence means 'Tell them something.' ☐
D. In many dialects, the sentence is correct and means the same as 'Don't tell them anything.' ☐
E. Nobody would ever say this sentence. ☐

8 Emphatic E, normal N or wrong W?

A. She was happy nowhere. ___
B. She wasn't happy anywhere. ___
C. Not anywhere was safe. ___
D. Nowhere was safe. ___

9 Right or wrong?

A. She didn't phone that day **or** the next day. ___
B. She didn't phone that day, **nor** the next day. ___
C. She didn't phone that day, **neither** the next day. ___ ▶

10 Right or wrong?

A. She hasn't got much chance, **I don't think.** ___
B. I wonder whether I **oughtn't** to go and see the doctor. ___

11 Right or wrong?

A. Somebody answer the phone, please. I'm busy. ___
B. You just sit down and relax for a bit. ___
C. You take your hands off me! ___

12 Right or wrong?

A. Don't you touch that bag or I'll call the police. ___
B. You don't touch that bag or I'll call the police. ___
C. Don't anybody say a word. ___
D. Anybody don't say a word. ___

18 linking words; verbs in subordinate clauses

1 Right R or wrong W?

A. I'm going to **try and eat** something. ___
B. I **tried and ate** something, but I couldn't manage. ___
C. I told her to **go and get** him from the station. ___
D. She **went and got** him from the station. ___
E. **Be sure and ask** Uncle Joe about the strawberries. ___
F. **Hurry up and open** the door. ___

2 Is the punctuation after *him* correct in these sentences? Why (not)?

I don't like **him**, but I agree that he's a good manager.
I don't like **him**; however, I agree that he's a good manager.

....

3 Right or wrong?

A. Just because you're older than me **doesn't mean** you can do what you like. ___
B. Just because you're older than me **it doesn't mean** you can do what you like. ___

4 Are these sentences right R, wrong W, or something in between B?

A. She both dances and she sings. ___
B. You'll either leave this house or I'll call the police. ___

5 Right or wrong?

A. He neither smiled, spoke nor looked at me. ___
B. Neither he smiled, spoke nor looked at me. ___

▶

6 Right or wrong?

A. **How you divide up the money** is your business. ☐
B. This is how **much I've done** since this morning. ☐
C. I spend my money **how I like**. ☐
D. Look at **how** those cats wash each other. ☐
E. Look at **the way how** those cats wash each other. ☐
F. Look at **the way** those cats wash each other. ☐

7 Right or wrong?

A. Tell me **immediately** you have any news. ☐
B. **Directly** I walked in the door, I could smell smoke. ☐
C. I loved you **the moment** I saw you. ☐

8 What do you think about these two sentences?
I'd rather like a cup of coffee.
I'd rather have a cup of coffee.

A. There is no significant difference. ☐
B. There is a slight difference of meaning. ☐
C. They mean completely different things. ☐
D. They mean the same, but there is a stylistic difference. ☐

9 Which of these sentences is/are possible in modern English?

A. I had rather you didn't. ☐
B. I had rather you wouldn't. ☐
C. I would rather you didn't. ☐
D. I would rather you wouldn't. ☐
E. I wouldn't rather go out tonight. ☐
F. I'd rather not go out tonight. ☐

10 What do you think about these two sentences?
They stayed awake all night **lest** there should be trouble.
They stayed awake all night **in case** there should be trouble.

A. There is no significant difference. ☐
B. There is a slight difference of meaning. ☐
C. They mean completely different things. ☐
D. They mean the same, but there is a stylistic difference. ☐

11 In which of these sentences would it be natural to leave out *that*?

A. He said **that** he was feeling better. ☐
B. James replied **that** he was feeling better. ☐
C. We were surprised **that** she came. ☐
D. There was strong opposition to Copernicus' theory **that** the earth went round the sun. ☐
E. Come in quietly so **that** she doesn't hear you. ☐

▶

12 Right or wrong?

I'll be surprised **unless** the car breaks down. ⌊___⌋

13 Right or wrong?

A. **Whether we can stay with my mother** is another matter. ⌊___⌋
B. **Whether I'm happy?** What do you think? ⌊___⌋

14 Put in appropriate discourse markers from the box. More than one may be possible in some cases. Not all the words and expressions in the box are used.

actually after all at least anyway certainly I mean in fact it's true that mind you of course sort of you know

A. The holiday was quite short. ...., we were only away for five days.
B. I really don't want to do it. It's not my kind of thing. ...., you can't make me, can you?
C. She phoned last Monday. ...., I think that's when it was.
D. The party was good, ..., it was sensational.
E. I've nothing against Conservatives. ...., I wouldn't want my daughter to marry one.
F. .... she was selfish, bad-tempered and unfaithful. But I loved her.
G. Why don't you come round at about, I don't know, maybe .... four o'clock, around then?
H. I don't remember whether it was Pete, Joe or Sebastian who told me. ...., it was one of those guys.

15 Present, future or both?

A. She's going to start out early so that she .... get stuck in rush-hour traffic. (*doesn't, won't*)
B. I'll get there as soon as you .... (*do, will*)
C. I'll probably have more trouble than you .... (*do, will*)
D. I don't know where I .... tomorrow. (*am, will be*)
E. I'll go where you .... (*go, will go*)
F. We all hope you .... better soon. (*get, will get*)
G. I bet Joe .... Frank in the semi-final. (*beats, will beat*)
H. I can't give your message to Anne because I .... see her until July. (*don't, won't*)
I. I'll give fifty euros to anyone who .... my coat. (*finds, will find*)
J. This is Mrs Andrews, who .... after the house when you're away next month. (*looks, will look*)

▶

16 Right or wrong?

A. In a really free country, you could say anything you **wanted to**. ☐
B. In a really free country, you could say anything you **would want to**. ☐
C. She would always give money to anybody who **needed** it. ☐
D. She would always give money to anybody who **would need** it. ☐

19 *if*

1 Right R or wrong W?

A. I'll give you £100 if **I will win** the lottery. ☐
B. I'll give you £100 if **it will help** you to go on holiday. ☐

2 Right or wrong?

A. If **Peter won't be** there this evening, there's no point in going to the meeting. ☐
B. I'm not sure if Peter's coming this evening. If **he won't be** there, I'll give the papers to his wife. ☐

3 What is the best description of this use of *will*?
If **you will eat** so much, it's not surprising you feel ill.

A. futurity ☐
B. possibility ☐
C. irritating habit ☐

4 Right or wrong?

A. If I **gave** you my address, would you write to me soon? ☐
B. If I **were to give** you my address, would you write to me soon? ☐
C. If I **knew** your address, I'd send you a postcard. ☐
D. If I **were to know** your address, I'd send you a postcard. ☐

5 Which two are right?

A. **If it hadn't been for** Sue, I don't know what I would have done. ☐
B. **If there hadn't been** Sue, I don't know what I would have done. ☐
C. **If Sue hadn't been**, I don't know what I would have done. ☐
D. **But for Sue**, I don't know what I would have done. ☐

6 What do you think about this sentence?
You want to get in, you pay like everybody else.

A. Normal and correct. ☐
B. Correct in an informal style. ☐
C. Incorrect. ☐

▶

7 How can we best describe these structures?

Were she my daughter, I would insist that she behave properly.
Had I realised the situation, I would have informed the police.
Should you change your mind, do not hesitate to contact me.

A. Normal and correct. ☐
B. Correct in a very formal style. ☐
C. Correct in an informal style. ☐
D. Incorrect. ☐

8 What does this spoken sentence probably mean?

I wouldn't be surprised if she didn't get married soon.

A. I'm not sure, but I think she may get married soon. ☐
B. I don't think she'll get married soon. ☐
C. I have no idea whether she'll get married soon. ☐

9 What is the best paraphrase of this sentence?

His style, if simple, is pleasant to read.

A. His style may or may not be simple. If it is, it's pleasant to read. ☐
B. His style is only pleasant to read when it's simple. ☐
C. His style is simple but it's pleasant to read. ☐

10 Are any of these sentences right?

A. How would we feel if this would happen to our family? ☐
B. If I'd have known, I'd have told you. ☐
C. If I knew you were coming, I'd have baked a cake. ☐

11 Grammar books often divide structures with *if* into three types: the so-called 'first, second and third conditionals'. How good is this analysis?

A. All structures with *if* can be explained in terms of these three sentence types. ☐
B. Some, but not all, structures with *if* can be explained in terms of these three sentence types. ☐
C. Structures with *if* can never be explained in terms of these three sentence types. ☐

20 indirect speech

1 Right R or wrong W?

A. We were glad to hear that you **enjoyed** your trip to Denmark. ⎵

B. We were glad to hear that you **had enjoyed** your trip to Denmark. ⎵

2 Which of these sentences are normal and correct?

A. The Greeks believed that the sun **goes** round the earth. ☐

B. The Greeks believed that the sun **went** round the earth. ☐

C. Copernicus proved that the earth **goes** round the sun. ☐

D. Copernicus proved that the earth **went** round the sun. ☐

3 Which are the right words to complete the indirect speech sentence?

DIRECT: It would be nice if I could see you again.

INDIRECT: He said it would be nice if he .... me again.

(*could see, could have seen, would see*)

4 Choose the right words to complete the indirect speech sentence.

DIRECT: Shall I be needed tomorrow?

INDIRECT: He wants to know if he .... be needed tomorrow.

(*shall, will, should, would*)

5 Choose the right words to complete the indirect speech sentence.

DIRECT: Shall I carry that bag?

INDIRECT: He wants to know if he .... carry that bag.

(*shall, will, should, would*)

6 What is the indirect speech equivalent of this sentence: A, B or both?

'If I had any money, I'd buy you a drink.'

A. She said if **she had** any money **she'd buy** me a drink. ☐

B. She said if **she'd had** any money **she'd have bought** me a drink. ☐

7 What is the indirect speech equivalent of this sentence?

'Isn't she lovely!'

A. I remarked how lovely she was. ☐

B. I exclaimed that she was lovely. ☐

C. I asked if she wasn't lovely. ☐

▶

Expert

8 **What is the indirect speech equivalent of this sentence: A, B or both?**
'Who's the best player?'

A. She asked me **who was the best player**. ☐
B. She asked me **who the best player was**. ☐

9 **One or both of these sentences is/are right. Which?**

A. This is the man who John said would tell us about the club. ☐
B. He's gone I don't know where. ☐

21 relatives

1 **Which of these is/are right?**

A. He's written a book **whose** name I've forgotten. ☐
B. He's written a book **the name of which** I've forgotten. ☐
C. He's written a book **that** I've forgotten **the name of.** ☐
D. He's written a book **of which** I've forgotten **the name**. ☐
E. He's married to a woman **of whom** I've forgotten **the name**. ☐

2 **What is the difference between these two sentences?**

A. I've got some friends **whose house** looks over a river.
B. I've got some friends **with a house that** looks over a river.

....

3 **Which sentence(s) is/are right?**

A. He lost his temper, **at which point** I decided to go home. ☐
B. He lost his temper, **which point** I decided to go home **at**. ☐
C. He lost his temper, **at what point** I decided to go home. ☐

4 **Right** R **or wrong** W**?**

A. I'll never forget **the day when** I first met you. ____
B. I'll never forget **the day** I first met you. ____
C. Do you know **a shop where** I can find sandals? ____
D. Do you know **a shop** I can find sandals? ____

5 **Right or wrong?**

A. The man **who I work for** is ill. ____
B. The man **for who I work** is ill. ____

6 **Right or wrong?**

A. This is for **whoever wants it**. ____
B. Take **whatever you want**. ____
C. I often think about **where I met you**. ____
D. Look at **how he treats me**! ____

▶

7 Right or wrong?

I rang Mrs Spencer up, who did our accounts. ___

8 Which of these sentences is/are right?

A. **It's me that am** responsible for the planning. ☐
B. **It's me that's** responsible for the planning. ☐
C. **It is I who am** responsible for the planning. ☐
D. **It is I who is** responsible for the planning. ☐

9 Which of these sentences is/are right?

A. I wish the children had a garden **in which to play**. ☐
B. I wish the children had a garden **which to play in**. ☐
C. I wish the children had a garden **to play in**. ☐

10 Right or wrong?

A. He's got **a new car that** goes like a bomb. ___
B. He's got **a new car, which** goes like a bomb. ___

11 Which sentence is right?

A. This is the woman **that Ann said could show** us the church. ☐
B. This is the woman **that Ann said that could show** us the church. ☐

12 Right or wrong?

I am enclosing an application form, **which I should be grateful if you would fill in and return**. ___

13 Right or wrong?

I was driving a car **that I didn't know how fast it would go**. ___

14 Right or wrong (in context)?

A. *[At a formal meeting]:* Is there anyone present wants to add any comments? ___
B. *[Kirsty MacColl song title]:* There's a guy works down the chip shop swears he's Elvis. ___

Expert

22 special sentence structures

1 Right R or wrong W?

A. **It's** wonderful the new concert hall. ___
B. **It's amazing** the way the architect planned it. ___
C. **It's amazing** the architect's vision. ___

2 Put in *it* or nothing (–) to make correct sentences.

A. We found .... tiring to listen to him.
B. I cannot bear .... to see people crying.
C. We love .... when you sing.
D. I take .... that you won't be working tomorrow.
E. I found .... strange being in her house.
F. We would appreciate .... if you would keep us informed.
G. We owe .... to society to help those who need help.
H. I'll leave .... to you to inform the other members.

3 Right or wrong?

I wondered **how reliable was the information** I had been given. ___

4 Right or wrong?

A. Not far from here **can you see** foxes. ___
B. Not only **did we lose** our money, we also wasted our time. ___
C. Under no circumstances **will I agree** to your conditions. ___

5 Which of these inversions are correct (in formal literary writing)?

A. Seldom **had I been** in such danger before. ☐
B. Sometimes **had I felt** frightened in the past. ☐
C. Only then **did I understand** how bad the situation was. ☐
D. Little **did I know** that I would soon be saved. ☐
E. Never **have I been** so glad to see someone arrive. ☐
F. Not for a moment **did she realise** the danger she was in. ☐
G. Not until he received her letter **did he fully understand** her feelings for him. ☐

6 Which sentence beginnings are possible?

... she went back out.

A. Cold though it was, ... ☐
B. Cold as it was, ... ☐
C. As cold as it was, ... ☐

7 Right or wrong?

Much as I respect your judgement, I think you're completely mistaken. ___

▶

8 What is the best explanation for the choice of structure in this sentence?

Margaret **had her roof blown off** in the storm.

A. Margaret is the main centre of interest, rather than the roof or the storm. ☐
B. Margaret had some responsibility herself for the damage. ☐
C. The damage took place before the main event that is about to be described. ☐
D. It would not be correct to begin with *The storm* ... in this sentence. ☐

9 Change the emphasis by reconstructing the sentence with different endings as shown.

What Mary kept in the bath was a goldfish.

A. .... was Mary.
B. .... was the bath.
C. .... was to keep a goldfish in the bath.

10 Right or wrong?

Why I'm here is to talk about my plans. ____

11 Right or wrong?

A. What he did was **scream**. ____
B. What he did was **to scream**. ____
C. What he did was, **he screamed**. ____

12 Right or wrong?

A. **This** is where you pay. ____
B. **Here** is where you pay. ____

13 Formal F, normal N or informal I?

A. It is I who am responsible. ____
B. It's me that's responsible. ____

14 Right or wrong?

A. Get up! ~ **I am**. ____
B. **If you can**, send me a postcard when you arrive. ____

15 Which of the replies is/are right?

Could you have been dreaming?

A. ~ I suppose I **could**. ☐
B. ~ I suppose I **could have**. ☐
C. ~ I suppose I **could have been**. ☐

▶

Expert

16 Which of the replies is/are right?

Do you think he'll phone?

A. ~ He **might.** ☐
B. ~ He **might do.** ☐

17 Right or wrong?

A. Are you and Gillian getting married? ~ **We hope.** ___
B. Are you and Gillian getting married? ~ **We hope to.** ___
C. There's more snow these days than there **used to.** ___
D. Do you want to go to University? ~ **I'd like.** ___
E. Stay as long as **you like.** ___

23 spoken grammar

1 Right R or wrong W?

A. I'm late, **aren't I**? ___
B. There's something wrong, **isn't there**? ___
C. Nobody phoned, **did they**? ___
D. So you're moving to London, **are you**? ___
E. This is the last bus, **is it**? ___
F. Have a good time, **did you**? ___

2 Put in the correct verbs from the ones in the box. More than one may be possible; not all of them can be used.

can	can't	could	couldn't	shall	will	won't	would	wouldn't

A. Do come in, ... you?
B. Give me a hand, ... you?
C. Don't forget, ... you?
D. Let's have a party, ... we?

3 Which of these is/are natural in speech?

A. I'll see you soon. ☐
B. Will see you soon. ☐
C. See you soon. ☐

4 Which of these are natural in speech?

A. You ready? ☐
B. She want something? ☐
C. I late? ☐
D. It raining? ☐
E. They back yet? ☐

▶

5 Which of these are natural in speech?

A. People like that I just can't stand. ☐
B. A lot of good that does me. ☐
C. What she wanted I never found out. ☐
D. Strange people they are! ☐
E. Last for ever, these shoes will. ☐

6 Is this spoken structure normal N, strange S or impossible I?

One of my brothers, his wife's a singer, he says it's really hard to make a living at it. ___

7 What about these: normal, strange or impossible?

A. Me, I don't care. ___
B. He hasn't a chance, Fred. ___
C. Hasn't a chance, Fred. ___
D. I don't think much of the party, me. ___
E. I don't think much of the party, myself. ___
F. Crazy, that driver. ___
G. Really got on my nerves, Sylvia did. ___
H. You've gone mad, you have. ___
I. You've gone mad, have you. ___

24 special kinds of English

1 How would you read this email address aloud?
p.watkins@kmail.co.uk

....

2 What does this text message mean?
tx 4 a gr8 party c u @ bbq @ 9

....

3 Can you compose a five-word newspaper headline to announce the following piece of news?
There has been a disagreement about a reduction in wages at a factory that makes furniture.

....

4 What does this newspaper headline mean?
TROOPS FOR GLASGOW?

....

▶

5 **The following headline appeared in the *Guardian* newspaper on 25 July, 2007. How close to it in meaning is the sentence below it?**

MINISTERS WARNED THREE YEARS AGO OVER FLOOD DEFENCE FAILINGS

Three years ago, ministers said that flood defences were unsatisfactory.

A. exactly the same ☐
B. close, but slightly different ☐
C. completely different ☐

6 **Right** R **or wrong** W**?**

A. **an** EU country ___
B. **a** MP ___
C. **a** US diplomat ___
D. **an** RAF pilot ___

7 **Right or wrong?**

A. **the** EU ___
B. **the** NATO ___
C. **the** CIA ___

8 **Can you rewrite this as it might appear in a recipe book?**

Pour the mixture into a large saucepan, heat it until it's boiling, then add three pounds of sugar and leave it on a low heat for 45 minutes.

....

....

25 social aspects of English; variation and change

1 **Imagine that a stranger, standing next to you in a queue, asks you to hold something for her for a moment. Would these ways of making the request be very polite** VP**, polite** P **or not polite** NP**?**

A. Hold this for me. ___
B. Please hold this for me. ___
C. You'd better hold this for me. ___
D. I wonder if you could possibly hold this for me? ___
E. Couldn't you hold this for me? ___
F. Could you possibly hold this for me? ___
G. You couldn't hold this for me, could you? ___
H. Would you mind holding this for me? ___

▶

Expert

2 Which of these are possible ways of asking for help?

A. **I hope** you can help me. ☐
B. **I'm hoping** you can help me. ☐
C. **I'll hope** you can help me. ☐
D. **I'll be hoping** you can help me. ☐
E. **I was hoping** you could help me. ☐
F. **I hoped** you could help me. ☐
G. **I would hope** you could help me. ☐

3 Which of these sentences might be said by a shop assistant in answer to a customer's enquiries?

A. How much **will you want** to spend, sir? ☐
B. How much **do you want** to spend, sir? ☐
C. How much **did you want** to spend, sir? ☐
D. **That will be** £37.50, sir. ☐
E. **That's** £37.50, sir. ☐
F. **That was** £37.50, sir. ☐

4 What does this mean?

This food's a bit expensive.

A. This food's not very expensive. ☐
B. This food costs more than it should. ☐
C. This food is just about the right price. ☐

5 Right R or wrong W?

A. How do you do? ~ **Fine, thanks.** ___
B. **Congratulation** on your exam result. ___
C. **Excuse me**, can I get past? ___
D. **I beg your pardon**. I didn't mean to push you. ___
E. Are you ready? ~ **I beg your pardon?** ~Are you ready? ___
F. Have a good journey. ___
G. You're welcome home. ___
H. Good appetite. ___
I. Have you got my tickets? ~ Yes, **here you are**. ___
J. Sleep well. ___

6 Which of these are possible alternatives to *Goodbye*?

A. Cheers. ☐
B. Take care. ☐
C. Hey, there. ☐
D. See you. ☐
E. See you later. ☐

▶

7 Which of these are possible replies to *Thank you*?

A. You're welcome. ☐
B. You're welcome to it. ☐
C. That's OK. ☐
D. (silence) ☐
E. No problem. ☐
F. Please. ☐
G. Not at all. ☐

8 Can you give the common British equivalents for these American English words?

A. catalog ....
B. pants ....
C. elevator ....
D. garbage ....
E. pavement ....
F. sidewalk ....
G. sneakers ....
H. faucet ....

9 Are these sentences: non-standard but correct in some dialects NS, standard but informal I, normal in standard English N or just wrong W?

A. The company has changed **it's** management. ⌴
B. **Alice and me** went to the same school. ⌴
C. I **ain't** done **nothing**. ⌴
D. There were **less people** than I expected. ⌴
E. **I wants them papers what I give** you yesterday. ⌴
F. I **could not understanding** the lecture. ⌴
G. One of the students hasn't sent back **their** registration form. ⌴
H. **Here's** those books you wanted. ⌴
I. **Seen John** anywhere? ⌴

10 Which of the two words or expressions is more formal than the other?

A. repair; mend ....
B. begin; commence ....
C. alight; get off ....

11 Which of these statements are true of modern English?

A. *Who* is replacing *whom*. ☐
B. *Will* is replacing *shall*. ☐
C. The present progressive is becoming less common. ☐
D. *If I were* is becoming less common. ☐
E. Comparatives with *more* are replacing some comparatives with *-er*. ☐
F. *Must* is replacing *have to*. ☐

▶

12 Which of these forms were correct in older English?

A. Alice **knowest** my mother very well. ☐
B. **Art thou** tired? ☐
C. Where is **thine** brother? ☐
D. **Came he** by sea or land? ☐
E. **Not be** afraid. ☐
F. Then **did he take** my hand. ☐
G. We **go not** out today. ☐

26 pronunciation

1 Where is the main stress on each of the following words?

A. photograph ....
B. photographer ....
C. photographic ....

2 Which words would be stressed in speech in the following sentence?

I asked for mashed potatoes, not fried potatoes.

....

3 Which words would normally be stressed in speech in the following sentence?

She was sure that the back of the car had been damaged.

....

4 Some common short English words have two pronunciations: a 'strong form', used when they are stressed, and a 'weak form', used when they are not stressed. For example, *for* can be pronounced like *four* (strong form) or like the end of *offer* (weak form). Which of the following words can have both strong and weak forms?

and at can have must of on off was were

....

5 Would the highlighted words normally be pronounced with strong S or weak W forms in these sentences?

A. What are you looking **at**? ____
B. I'm looking **at** you. ____
C. I **must** go now. ____
D. Yes, you **must**. ____
E. This is **for** Andrew. ____
F. You **were** late again this morning. ____
G. Perhaps you **can** help me with this. ____
H. It **was**n't me. ____

▶

6 Which of these statements is/are true?

A. *Going to* is often pronounced like *gonna*. ☐
B. *Got to* is often pronounced like *gotta*. ☐
C. *Went to* is often pronounced like *wenna*. ☐
D. *Want to* is often pronounced like *wanna*. ☐
E. *Have to* is often pronounced like *hafta*. ☐
F. *Mean to* is often pronounced like *meana*. ☐

27 numbers

1 How do you say these numbers?

A. 3⁄7 ....
B. 317⁄524 ....
....
C. 0.375 ....
D. 7⁄10 litre ....
E. 0.6 cm ....

2 Which is right?

A. one and a half **hour** ☐
B. one and a half **hours** ☐

3 Right R or wrong W?

A. Three quarters of a ton **are** too much. ___
B. A third of the students **are** from abroad. ___
C. One in three new cars **break** down in the first year. ___

4 How do you say '0' in the following?

A. 3–0 (football match result) ....
B. 40–0 (score in a tennis game) ....
C. 0 degrees (temperature) ....
D. 0163 07626 (phone number) ....

5 Right or wrong?

A. Hamlet dies in **the fifth act.** ___
B. Hamlet dies in **Act 5**. ___
C. **Henry Eight** had six wives. ___
D. **Henry Eighth** had six wives. ___

6 What are the American English equivalents of the following British expressions?

A. the ground floor ....
B. the first floor ....

▶

7 How might these numbers be said differently in British and American English?

A. 310 ....

B. 5,642 ....

8 In which of these numbers is it possible to say 'a' instead of 'one'?

A. 100 ☐
B. 1000 ☐
C. 1,642 ☐
D. 1,027 ☐
E. 3,196 ☐

9 Right or wrong?

A. several **thousand** euros ___
B. several **thousands** euros ___
C. several **thousands of** euros ___
D. six two-**hours** lessons ___
E. How tall is he? ~ Six **foot** four. ___

10 What are the approximate metric equivalents?

A. one pound: 0.6kg, 1.2kg, 2.2kg or 4kg ....

B. one foot: 18cm, 24cm, 30cm or 48cm ....

C. one mile: 0.8km, 1.6km, 1.9km or 2.55km ....

D. one acre: 0.4 hectares, 0.9 hectares, 2 hectares or 7.6 hectares

....

11 Right or wrong?

A. There are twelve of us in my family. ___
B. We are twelve in my family. ___

12 Which of these is/are right?

A. Two and two is four. ☐
B. Two and two are four. ☐
C. Two and two equals four. ☐
D. Two and two equal four. ☐

13 What would be a natural way of saying this?

3 x 4 = 12 ....

14 Which of these is/are right?

A. Seventeen multiplied by thirty-five equals five hundred and eighty-five. ☐
B. Seventeen times thirty-five equals five hundred and eighty-five. ☐
C. Seventeen times thirty-five is five-hundred and eighty-five. ☐
D. Seventeen times thirty-five are five-hundred and eighty-five. ☐

Expert

28 words (1): similar words

1 Is *alright*:

A. all right? ☐
B. all wrong? ☐
C. common but not accepted by everybody? ☐

2 Match the words with the definitions or comments.

alone lonely lonesome lone

A. suggests unhappiness (British and American English) ....
B. not generally used before nouns ....
C. rather literary ....
D. suggests unhappiness (more common in American English) ....

3 *Classic* or *classical*?

A. Sophocles was the greatest .... dramatist.
B. He's a .... example of an old-style hippy.
C. Do you like .... music?
D. There's a .... car museum in Epsom.

4 *South* or *southern*?

A. She's got a beautiful .... accent.
B. My room's on the .... side of the house.
C. What's the capital of .... Africa?
D. Most of this country's population is concentrated in the .... counties.
E. We spent our holiday on the .... coast.

5 *Electric* or *electrical*?

A. Ann's studying .... engineering.
B. As the President rose to speak, the atmosphere was ....
C. I need a new .... shaver.

6 *Especially*, *specially* or both?

A. It wasn't .... hot last summer.
B. We all like music – my father ....
C. These shoes were .... made for me. ▶

7 *Historic* or *historical*?

A. Was King Arthur a .... figure?
B. The two countries have signed a .... agreement.
C. Scotland is full of .... castles and houses.
D. Do you ever read .... novels?

8 *Magic, magical* or both?

A. If we had a .... carpet we could get through this traffic.
B. Mum, can I have an ice-cream? ~ What's the .... word? ~ Please.
C. We spent a .... evening together, just sitting by the river and talking.

9 *Policy* or *politics*?

A. She's studying British colonial .... in the 18th century.
B. You talk beautifully: you should be in ....
C. It's my .... to disbelieve all politicians.

10. Right R or wrong W?

A. Wake! It's time to go to work. [ ]
B. I woke up three times in the night. [ ]
C. I woke three times in the night. [ ]
D. The prince wakened her with a kiss. [ ]

29 words (2): other confusable words

1 Right R or wrong W?

A. **They don't allow to make** personal phone calls from the office. [ ]
B. **It is not allowed to make** personal phone calls from the office. [ ]
C. **We are not allowed to make** personal phone calls from the office. [ ]
D. The children **are not allowed out** at night. [ ]
E. We got to the theatre at 6.00, but we **were only let in** at 6.30. [ ]

2 *Besides, except, apart from* or all three?

A. .... the violin, she also plays the trombone.
B. I work every day .... Thursdays.
C. He has nothing .... his salary. ▶

Expert

3 One or more of the words in brackets is/are right in each case. Which?

A. Please .... ready now. (*become, get*)
B. I'm .... more and more impatient. (*becoming, getting*)
C. How did that window .... broken? (*become, get*)
D. She's looking forward to .... a grandmother. (*becoming, getting*)
E. I think that meat has .... bad. (*got, gone*)
F. May all your dreams .... true. (*get, come, turn*)
G. I don't want to .... old. (*get, grow*)
H. When she's embarrassed she always .... red. (*gets, goes, turns*)

4 *Get*, *go* or both?

A. I'm not sure I can .... over that wall.
B. I usually .... to Bristol by car.
C. There was a lot of traffic, and I only managed to .... to the meeting at 8.30.

5 *Also*, *as well*, and/or *too*?

A. She plays the piano and .... the flute.
B. She plays the piano and the flute ....
C. He's been to Peru, and I have ....
D. I'm fed up. ~ Me ....

6 Which of these is/are correctly punctuated? Why?

A. I don't like **him. However**, I agree that he's a good manager. ☐
B. I don't like **him; however**, I agree that he's a good manager. ☐
C. I don't like **him, however**, I agree that he's a good manager. ☐

7 When can you use *though* but not *although*?

....

8 *Because*, *as* and *since* can all be used to introduce causes or reasons. How is *because* different from the other two?

A. Unlike *because*, *as* and *since* are used most often when the reason is not the most important part of the information given in the sentence. ☐
B. Unlike *as* and *since*, *because* can be used when there is no time-reference in the sentence. ☐
C. *Because* makes the reason more persuasive than *as* or *since*. ☐

▶

9 Right or wrong?

A. While I **sat** reading the paper, Penny **cooked** lunch. ____
B. While I **was sitting** reading the paper, Penny **was cooking** lunch. ____
C. As the fire **died** down, Angela **drifted** off to sleep. ____
D. As the fire **was dying** down, Angela **was drifting** off to sleep. ____

10 Right or wrong?

A. What time **do you expect** her to phone? ____
B. What time **are you expecting** her to phone? ____
C. I **expect** she'll phone about 6.00. ____
D. **I'm expecting** she'll phone about 6.00. ____
E. I hope John **doesn't miss** the train. ____
F. I hope John **won't miss** the train. ____

11 (British English) Which film is best? Which is least good?

Film A is **quite good**. Film B is **rather good**. Film C is **fairly good**.

....

12 Which is/are right?

A. It's **quite a** good film. ☐
B. It's **rather a** good film. ☐
C. It's **fairly a** good film. ☐

13 *If*, *in case* or both?

You should phone 999 .... there's a fire.

14 Which is/are right?

A. I **no more** support the Labour Party. ☐
B. I **no longer** support the Labour Party. ☐
C. I **don't** support the Labour Party **any more**. ☐
D. I **don't** support the Labour Party **any longer**. ☐

15 Which one is wrong? Why?

A. JOHN: It's more expensive to travel on Friday.
SUE: **So** I'll leave on Thursday. ☐
B. JOHN: It's more expensive to travel on Friday.
SUE: **Then** I'll leave on Thursday. ☐
C. SUE: It's more expensive to travel on Friday; **so** I'll leave on Thursday. ☐
D. SUE: It's more expensive to travel on Friday; **then** I'll leave on Thursday. ☐

▶

16 Right or wrong (in British English)?

A. Can you **bring** the car to the garage tomorrow? I won't have time.
B. I'll arrive at the station at 6.00. Can you **take** the car and pick me up?
C. Where's that report? ~ I **brought** it to you when you were in the boardroom.
D. We're going out to dinner tonight. Would you like to join us and **bring** your girlfriend?

17 Right or wrong?

A. Ann's back in London. I'm going to **come** and see her at the weekend.
B. Can you **come** and see me in my office tomorrow?
C. We're going to the cinema tonight. Would you like to **come** with us?
D. He waited for her till six o'clock, but she didn't **come**.

18 Right or wrong?

A. I'm used to drive in London now, but it was hard at the beginning.
B. You'll soon get used to living in the country.

30 words (3): other vocabulary problems

1 Right R or wrong W?

A. It's over 100 kilos. Let me look. Yes, the **actual** weight is 108 kilos.
B. He said he was 40, but his **actual** age was 48.
C. Did you enjoy your holiday? ~ Very much, **actually**.
D. In 1900, the population of London was higher than it is **actually**.
E. She was so angry that she **actually** tore up the letter.
F. Hello, John. Nice to see you. ~ **Actually**, my name's Andy.

2 Right or wrong?

A. Can you go **any faster**?
B. The weather's **no different** from yesterday.
C. The weather's **no better** than yesterday.
D. Was the film **any good**?

3 Right or wrong?

A. I'll get a job one of these days. But **before**, I want to travel.
B. When I went back to the town I had left eight years **before**, everything was different.
C. When I went back to the town I had left **before** eight years, everything was different.
D. I think I've seen this film **before**.

4 Is/are any of these sentences wrong? If so, rewrite it/them.

A. **I doubt whether** interest rates will rise.

....

B. **I doubt if** she'll come this evening.

....

C. **We doubt that** new investment is needed.

....

D. **I doubt** we'll have enough money for a holiday.

....

5 Right or wrong?

A. He was driving **fast indeed.** ____
B. He was driving **quite fast indeed.** ____
C. It's cold. ~ It is **indeed.** ____

6 Which of these can *just* mean?

A. At or around this moment. ☐
B. Only, scarcely, nothing more than. ☐
C. Nearly. ☐
D. Exactly. ☐
E. Today. ☐

7 Which of these is/are correct?

A. **I telephoned** Ann just now. ☐
B. **I've telephoned** Ann just now. ☐
C. **I** just now **telephoned** Ann. ☐
D. **I've** just now **telephoned** Ann. ☐

8 Which of these can *miss* mean?

A. Be without. ☐
B. Notice the absence of. ☐
C. Be sorry to be without. ☐
D. Fail to contact, be late for. ☐

9 Which of these sentences is/are correct, if any?

A. No matter what you do is fine with me. ☐
B. I'll always love you, no matter what. ☐
C. No matter when you come. ☐

10 Is this reply all right?

It's cold. ~ **Of course it is.**

....

▶

11 Right R, wrong W or something in between B?

A. **The reason that** I came here was to be with my family. ⎵

B. **The reason why** I came here was to be with my family. ⎵

C. **The reason** I came here was to be with my family. ⎵

D. **The reason why** I came here was **because** I wanted to be with my family. ⎵

E. **The reason why** I came here was **that** I wanted to be with my family. ⎵

12 Is this informal reply right or wrong? If it's wrong, correct it.

How are you feeling? ~ **So-and-so.** ⎵

....

13 What is the best explanation for this use of *surely*?

Surely that's your mother over there.

A. I think that's your mother (but perhaps it seems surprising). ☐

B. That's certainly your mother. ☐

14 Which is/are correct: A, B or both?

A. **Something's the matter** with my foot. ☐

B. **There's something the matter** with my foot. ☐

15 Which of these sentences suggest(s) that the speaker's belief was right?

A. I THOUGHT Ann would phone. ☐

B. I thought Ann would PHONE. ☐

C. I HAD thought Ann would phone. ☐

16 Right or wrong in standard British English?

A. The car wants cleaned. ⎵

B. The car wants cleaning. ⎵

C. The car wants a clean. ⎵

17 Which of these sentences is/are correct?

A. I wish I spoke French. ☐

B. I wish I were better looking. ☐

C. I wish you would go home. ☐

D. I wish you weren't leaving so soon. ☐

E. I wish I felt better tomorrow. ☐

F. I wish you wouldn't drive so fast. ☐

G. I wish you didn't drive so fast. ☐

▶

Expert

18 Right or wrong?

A. The car isn't worth repairing. ☐
B. It isn't worth repairing the car. ☐
C. The car isn't worth repairing it. ☐
D. The car isn't worth to be repaired. ☐